The Last Mile to Quality Service Delivery in Jordan

DIRECTIONS IN DEVELOPMENT
Human Development

The Last Mile to Quality Service Delivery in Jordan

Tamer Samah Rabie, Samira Nikaein Towfighian, Cari Clark, and Melani Cammett

WORLD BANK GROUP

Contents

Acknowledgments   *ix*
Abbreviations   *xi*

| | Executive Summary | 1 |

Chapter 1	Accountability and Quality of Service Delivery	7
	Introduction	7
	Accountability and Provider Effort	8
	Motivation of the Present Report	14
	Report Roadmap	15
	Notes	15
	References	16

Chapter 2	Education Quality, Teacher Effort, and Accountability	21
	Introduction	21
	The Education Sector in Jordan	27
	Principal Monitoring and Teacher Effort	29
	Monitoring, Teacher Effort, and Student Learning in Jordan	42
	Comparative Case Study in Jordanian Schools	50
	Conclusions	54
	Notes	54
	References	55

Chapter 3	Healthcare Quality, Provider Effort, and Accountability	59
	Introduction	59
	The Health Sector in Jordan	66
	CMO Monitoring and Provider Effort	71
	Conclusions	85
	Notes	85
	References	85

Chapter 4   Conclusions and Policy Recommendations   89
              Notes   97
              References   98

Appendix A   Education Sector   99

Appendix B   Sensitivity Analysis   105

Appendix C   Health Sector   107

Boxes

2.1   Sampling   30
2.2   Limitations of the Principal Monitoring Index   33
2.3   Caveat for Teacher Effort Measures   36
2.4   Bivariate Correlations among Measures of Teacher Effort   36
2.5   Multilevel Mediation Analysis   43
2.6   Robustness Check and Sensitivity Analysis   49

Figures

2.1   Public Education Expenditure as a Share of Total Government
        Expenditure and Average PISA Math Scores   28
2.2   Principal Monitoring Measures   32
2.3   Principal Monitoring Index   32
2.4   Measures of Teacher Effort Mapped against the FFT   34
2.5   Creating an Environment of Respect and Rapport   36
2.6   Providing Feedback to Students   38
2.7   Designing Student Assessments   38
2.8   Designing Coherent Instruction   39
2.9   Causal Pathways of Principal Monitoring on Student Learning 43
2.10   Letter Sound Knowledge   45
2.11   Reading Comprehension   46
2.12   Number Identification   46
2.13   Word Problems   47
3.1   Life Expectancy: Jordan, MENA Average, and Selected
        Other Countries, 1980–2011   67
3.2   Infant Mortality versus Income and Total Health Spending, 2011   68
3.3   Maternal Mortality Relative to Income and Spending, 2010   69
3.4   Total Health Expenditure as a Share of GDP and Income
        Per Capita, 2011   70
3.5   Relationship between Monitoring and Rights-Based Care,
        by Sanction Level   83
B.1   Sensitivity Analysis Results   106

Tables

2.1	Study Instruments	31
2.2	Measures of Teacher Effort	35
2.3	Correlation between Measures of Teacher Effort	37
2.4	Control Variables	40
2.5	Substantive Effects—Principal Monitoring and Teacher Effort	41
2.6	Measures of Student Outcomes	47
2.7	Control Variables Included in the Mediation Analysis	48
3.1	Number of Primary Health Facilities Sampled by Governorate	73
3.2	Contents of Data Collection Instruments	74
3.3	Measures of Provider Effort	75
3.4	Measures of Within-Facility Accountability	76
3.5	Potential Confounding Factors	77
3.6	Percentage of Healthcare Providers Following CPGs	79
3.7	Percentage of Providers Practicing Rights-Based Care	80
3.8	Correlations between Indicators of Provider Effort	80
3.9	Correlations between Within-Facility and Top-Down and Bottom-Up Measures of Accountability	82
A.1	Framework for Teaching	99
A.2	Summary Statistics	100
A.3	Principal Monitoring and Teacher Effort in Jordan	101
A.4	Summary Statistics of Variables Included in the Mediation Analysis	103
A.5	The Indirect Effect of Principal Monitoring on Student Outcomes	103
A.6	Robustness Checks on the Indirect Effect of Principal Monitoring on Student Outcomes	103
C.1	Relationship between Accountability Practices and Provider Effort	108

Acknowledgments

This book is the product of the collaborative effort by a core team led by Tamer Samah Rabie and comprises Samira Nikaein Towfighian, Cari Clark, and Melani Cammett.

The authors sincerely appreciate the strategic guidance and support of Ferid Belhaj, Ernest Massiah, Safaa El Tayeb El-Kogali, Hana Brixi, Pilar Maisterra, Tania Meyer, and Haneen Ismail Sayed.

This work would have not been possible without the distinguished collaboration and warm hospitality of government officials at the Ministry of Planning and International Cooperation, the Ministry of Education, the Ministry of Health, and the High Health Council of the Hashemite Kingdom of Jordan. The authors are especially grateful to Rajaa Khater, Firyal Aqel, Feda Jaradat, and Ikram Khasawneh for their most valuable insights and comments. The authors are also thankful to all members of the Technical Advisory Committee, who provided excellent guidance and support throughout this study.

The authors are greatly indebted to Alan Potter and Brett Casper for their most capable research assistantship, and to Son Nam Nguyen and Dina Abu-Ghaida for their very helpful comments in their capacity as peer reviewers. The authors are especially thankful to Ellen Lust for her significant intellectual contribution at the early stages of this study. The authors are also thankful to Samira Halabi for her contributions.

This report also benefited from the administrative support of Fatima-Ezzahra Mansouri and Mariam Wakim, the editorial work of Amy Gautam, and data collection efforts of the Dajani Consulting team.

The authors are very grateful to the United States Agency for International Development and to RTI International for the design and implementation of the Early Grade Reading Assessment, Early Grade Math Assessment, and the Snapshot of School Management Effectiveness tools, and for sharing their datasets.

Finally, the authors are thankful to the MENA Multi-Donor Trust Fund (MDTF) for funding this work and for their support. The MENA MDTF is funded by the governments of Denmark, Finland, Norway, and the United Kingdom of Great Britain and Northern Ireland.

Abbreviations

CHC	community health committee
CHCC	comprehensive health center
CLASS	Classroom Assessment Scoring System
CMO	chief medical officer
CPG	clinical practice guideline
EGMA	Early Grade Math Assessment
EGRA	Early Grade Reading Assessment
EMIS	Education Management Information System
FFT	Framework for Teaching
GDP	gross domestic product
HCAC	Healthcare Accreditation Council
JD	Jordanian dinar
MENA	Middle East and North Africa
MOH	Ministry of Health
NCD	noncommunicable disease
OECD	Organisation for Economic Co-operation and Development
PHCC	primary healthcare center
PISA	Program for International Student Assessment
PMS	performance management system
RMS	Royal Medical Service
SD	standard deviation
SI	sequential ignorability
TIMSS	Trends in International Mathematics and Science Study
USAID	United States Agency for International Development

Executive Summary

International Evidence Calls for Greater Attention to Provider Effort to Improve Quality of Education and Healthcare Service Delivery

In many developing countries, governments have invested substantial resources in the provision of basic services such as healthcare and education. However, these investments frequently yield minimal improvements in student learning and health outcomes. One reason can be found in a growing body of research that suggests investment in the structural dimensions of service quality beyond a certain threshold is unlikely to improve service delivery outcomes. Indeed, the quantity and quality of structural determinants of education and healthcare services such as infrastructure, classroom and medical supplies, and even teacher and medical training are largely irrelevant if teachers and healthcare providers do not exert the requisite effort to translate these inputs into effective teaching and medical service. In essence, providers must exert adequate levels of effort by coming to work regularly and complying with technical and professional standards to provide high-quality education and healthcare services.

Promoting Adequate Provider Effort Necessitates Accountability, Including Effective Within-Facility Accountability: The Focus of This Report

To exert adequate effort, providers must feel that they are accountable for the quality of service they provide. Yet, a sense of accountability among providers does not necessarily occur naturally, often requiring mechanisms to monitor and incentivize provider effort. These mechanisms can come from the top down, bottom up, or within a facility. As the name implies, *top-down accountability* aims at promoting provider effort through government oversight. *Bottom-up accountability* gives citizens the means to directly hold providers accountable. Both of these approaches play an important role in improving provider accountability. In the accountability framework, the role of supervisors in the facilities where service provision occurs has thus far been underemphasized. By capitalizing on the technical knowledge of supervisors in health centers and schools and on their proximity to the actual service delivery exchange, within-facility accountability may be able to overcome some of the limitations of top-down and bottom-up mechanisms, substantially contributing to improved provider accountability.

This book contributes to addressing this underemphasis, specifically focusing on the linkages between within-facility accountability and provider effort in the health and education sectors in Jordan. In the case of healthcare, a study was developed to generate novel insights from an original survey instrument. It is worth noting that this is the first nationally representative study in Jordan to measure within-facility accountability and provider effort in primary health care facilities, and the first study in the Middle East and North Africa region to investigate these linkages. The study relies on a nationally representative sample of 122 primary healthcare facilities where data are collected through patient exit interviews, and surveys administered to chief medical officers, doctors, and nurses who work at the centers, and where available, a representative of the community health committee. In the case of education, an empirical analysis of a nationally representative sample of 156 schools was conducted, relying on existing data collected through principal, teacher, and student surveys; third-party classroom observations and school inventories; and math and reading student assessments. This empirical analysis was complemented by a comparative case study of six Jordanian schools using statistical matching and a process-tracing procedure.

Jordan Provides an Excellent Case to Study the Role of Accountability in Improving the Quality of Education and Healthcare Service Delivery

In the past two decades, Jordan has achieved close to universal primary school enrollment (97 percent) and completion (93 percent), as well as high enrollment (88 percent) and completion (90 percent) rates at the secondary level, on par with Organisation for Economic Co-Operation and Development (OECD) countries. Yet, international student assessments refocus the country's attention on what actually matters: student learning. Despite high levels of educational attainment, 15-year-old Jordanians' average mathematics, language, and science Program for International Student Assessment (PISA) scores rank among the lowest of PISA-participating countries. Similarly, in education systems that participate in the Trends in International Mathematics and Science (TIMSS) Study, eighth-grade students' average achievement in both mathematics and science ranks at nearly the bottom. Indicators as such are somewhat unexpected given Jordan's internationally comparable expenditure levels in the education sector. Public education expenditure as a share of total government expenditure stood at roughly 10.3 percent in 2012, slightly above the OECD average for that same year (9.8 percent), and on par with, for example, strong PISA performers such as Austria, Germany, and Poland. Furthermore, public education expenditure as a share of GDP was 3.4 percent in 2011, just below the OECD average (5.2 percent), and yet at the same level as the top PISA performers: Japan; Singapore; Macao SAR, China; and Hong Kong SAR, China.

Similarly, remarkable progress in improving the health status of the population has been made in the past two decades. Life expectancy at birth increased from 69.9 years in 1990 to 73.7 years in 2012; maternal mortality declined from 86 per 100,000 live births in 1990 to 50 in 2013; infant mortality reduced from 34 per 1,000 live births from 1990 to 17 in 2012; and the under-5 mortality rate declined from 39 per 1,000 live births to 21 in the same time period. Despite these gains, Jordan's health indicators, especially infant and maternal mortality, suggest that considerable health gains can be made in quality of care. Although it may be concluded that the underlying dynamics for the perceived inadequate quality of services in Jordan are fueled by limited resources going into the system, the evidence suggests otherwise. In 2011, Jordan's public spending on health as a percentage of GDP stood at approximately 6 percent, almost double that of the Middle East and North Africa average. This was mirrored in per capita health expenditures, which stood at US$392. This is well above the averages for low- and middle-income countries and for developing countries in the Middle East and North Africa region, although it is not the highest in the region. Jordan stands out in the region and among countries of similar economies more generally for its high levels of public health spending.

The evident contrast between (a) Jordan's adequate spending on education and healthcare services and (b) the somewhat inadequate levels of student learning and health outcomes achieved by the country suggests that the quality production function in Jordan is not constrained by structural inputs, but rather by limitations on how providers translate inputs into services. Thus, this study seeks to understand how within-facility accountability mechanisms can be used to improve service delivery in a country where structural inputs are largely already in place, providing a valuable case study for countries in the Middle East and North Africa as well as in other regions.

Evidence from Jordanian Schools and Primary Healthcare Centers Reveals That Effort Put Forth by Teachers and Healthcare Providers in Their Jobs Is Seemingly Low

Taking into consideration existing education data, this study identifies four substantive measures of teacher effort that are aligned with teachers' professional standards in Jordan, as stipulated by Jordan's Civil Service Bureau. Teachers are expected to strive to (a) provide continuous feedback to students; (b) respond to students' questions in a way that is conducive to creating a respectful and emotionally supportive environment for learning; (c) design a range of student assessment methods that provide a variety of performance opportunities for students; and (d) consider specific student performance and needs while designing lessons. The study finds that effort put forth by teachers in meeting these standards is seemingly low. Only one in five teachers marks all pages of students' copybooks, whereas roughly 25 percent of teachers mark only a few pages, and 3.4 percent do not mark even a single page. When students are unable to answer a question, they report that as many as 70 percent of teachers simply repeat the exact same question or ask another student instead, whereas 5.4 percent of teachers scold the student or send him or her outside of the classroom or to stand in a corner. Moreover, almost two in three teachers report using only one or two methods of student assessment and as little as one in four of all teachers report using these assessments to inform their lesson planning. Although these findings are exclusive to teachers in early primary grades, they may be indicative of a wider challenge present across education levels in Jordan.

Findings from the analysis of the original data collected in the primary health-care sector similarly show provider effort (measured as absenteeism, the expenditure of clinical effort during a patient encounter, the amount of time spent with patients, and the provision of rights-based care) is low in multiple areas. During field visits to health centers, 17 percent of health providers on average were reported absent (both excused and unexcused). On average, 17 percent absenteeism is better than studies have found in other similarly developed countries. However, the average represents substantial variation across facilities. Although some clinics were operating fully staffed, others were missing more than half of their providers, suggesting a lack of access to care. On the basis of interviews conducted with patients exiting healthcare facilities, study findings highlight low provider effort during the clinical encounter. On average, health providers performed only half of key exam elements, suggesting that diagnoses and other health-related decisions are made with limited clinical information. Furthermore, these decisions occur during clinical encounters that last as little as 4 minutes. The average length of an encounter was 10 minutes, but thorough, high-quality, rights-based care is difficult to deliver in the span of 10 minutes, let alone 4. The data substantiated that shorter encounters were associated with lower clinical effort and a lower likelihood of the provision of rights-based care; however, on average, patients reported that they received respectful, responsive, rights-based care.

Increasing Principal and Chief Medical Officer Monitoring May Yield Tangible Improvements in Provider Effort in the Workplace

School principals and chief medical officers are well placed to identify low levels of provider effort when they see them, given that they are trained as teachers and medical doctors, have spent numerous years teaching in the classroom and providing clinical services, and share the same workspace as do the teachers and healthcare providers they oversee. This study provides new evidence about the critical role that school principals and chief medical officers can play in strengthening provider accountability and assisting teachers and healthcare providers to exert the effort needed to provide quality services.

This education study finds that principal monitoring—as measured by a constructed composite index of monitoring practices—is a strong predictor of teacher effort but that the effect of principal monitoring is a function of principals' ability to observe teacher effort in a given effort area. Furthermore, the study reveals that principal monitoring is strongly associated with student learning, and that such association is mediated by those areas of teacher effort that are observable to the principal. Findings in the health sector mimic those in educa-tion. Health providers exert greater effort in examining and treating patients and spend more time with patients when chief medical officers institute and conduct monitoring procedures at the facility level.

Reaping the Highest Values from Principal and Chief Medical Officer Monitoring Necessitates a Strong Incentives Environment

Despite the effort gains that are possible through appropriate monitoring, the accountability environment in Jordan's education and health sectors provides very few incentives for teachers and healthcare providers to exert the highest level of effort possible. On the one hand, financial incentives to encourage pro-vider effort are absent. At the central level, salary schemes for teachers and healthcare providers are tied only to providers' credentials and years of experi-ence, providing no incentive for providers to perform to their full potential knowledge capacity. At the facility level, principals' and chief medical officers' limited managerial autonomy and constrained facility budgets preclude the use of financial incentives, whereas their inability to hire and fire staff limits the effect of their efforts to bolster provider accountability. On the other hand, principals and chief medical officers in Jordan seldom rely on nonfinan-cial mechanisms to incentivize provider effort. When they do, they make use mostly of mechanisms to sanction, largely underusing the potential of positive nonfinancial incentives.

The Move toward Performance-Based Education and Health Systems in Jordan Is Imperative

The largely adequate structural inputs in Jordan's education and health sectors stand in sharp contrast with the seemingly low effort exerted by teachers and healthcare providers, significantly hindering the country's ability to provide high-quality services. This calls for a move toward performance-based education and health systems in Jordan, whereby provider accountability is put at the heart of each sector's reform agenda. Moving toward such performance-based account-ability systems requires Jordan to ponder four key considerations: (a) the need to select and establish adequate indicators to measure provider performance; (b) the requirement to standardize and systematize the collection of perfor-mance indicators; (c) the need to design and tie effective rewards and sanctions schemes to performance indicators to incentivize high provider effort; and (d) the need to institute mechanisms that keep principals and chief medical officers accountable and providing the necessary training and managerial auton-omy to allow them to better perform their supervisory roles are required to champion such an important undertaking across the country. Doing so requires a systems approach that integrates performance-based accountability into a larger performance management system in which performance indicators inform the design of strategic professional development opportunities for providers.

The Last Mile to Quality Service Delivery in Jordan • http://dx.doi.org/10.1596/978-1-4648-1069-5

Accountability and Quality of Service Delivery

Introduction

In many developing countries, governments have invested vast resources in the provision of basic services such as healthcare and education. Public health facilities and schools now extend across national territories even in rural areas. In many countries, a booming private sector has emerged to compete with public services, at least for those consumers who can afford them. As a result, citizens enjoy unprecedented access to basic services, particularly in middle-income countries. But the provision of healthcare and education does not guarantee that people receive the correct diagnoses and treatment they require, or develop the literacy, numeracy, and other life skills that they need to become productive and informed members of society. In many countries, this is because the quality of social services presents distinct challenges that prohibit citizens from obtaining their *de jure* entitlements to basic schooling or healthcare in the public sector.

At the most fundamental level, the quality of healthcare or education can be disaggregated into several dimensions related to the structure, process, and outcome of the delivery of services (Donabedian 1988; RAND 2012). The structural dimension of quality refers to the material and human resources and the physical and organizational characteristics of the facility where service delivery occurs (Donabedian 1988). This includes the availability and condition of relevant equipment, the level of training among staff members, inputs, supplies, and appropriate infrastructure up and down the supply chain. The process-oriented component of quality includes the technical and interpersonal processes through which services are provided (Donabedian 1988). Process measures assess the degree to which staff members apply their technical knowledge to deliver the service in question in an appropriate and responsive manner, and the extent of provider adherence to guidelines or standards specific to the service delivery type. Last, outcome measures of quality denote the results of the service exchange. This can include intermediate outcomes, such as utilization of healthcare services or enrollment rates for schools, as well as metrics to capture physical and financial access to services (Roberts and others 2008). In addition, at the far end of the spectrum, quality outcomes include human development outcomes such as the health status of patients, student learning, and client satisfaction.

A growing body of research on the quality of both health and education suggests that prioritizing investment in the structural dimensions of quality beyond a certain threshold or ceiling is likely to yield minimal benefits for health and educational outcomes (Cristia and others 2012; Das and Hammer 2014; Glewwe and others 2004; Hanushek 2003; RAND 2012). In other words, while investments in physical and organizational structures are needed and desirable, concentrating only on these dimensions and ignoring the incentive environment and its influence on what actually happens in patient-provider or student-teacher interactions will ultimately produce minimal gains in patient health outcomes or student learning (Hanushek 2003; Mitchell and others 1998). Many developing countries have already invested substantially in the social sectors and yet human development outcomes have not improved at a commensurate rate (Das and Hammer 2014; Glewwe and others 2013; RAND 2012). The real challenges to health and educational systems relate to quality of service delivery, which is less easily measured than expenditures and, as noted above, plays a key role in improving outcomes (World Bank 2003). This calls for a shift in emphasis from *having the right things*—structures—to *doing the right things*—processes—to *having the right things happen*—outcomes (Mitchell and others 1998).

Doing the right things requires that teachers and healthcare providers come to work regularly, comply with technical and professional standards, and exert sufficient effort to ensure that community members receive the services required to meet their needs. This assumes a certain level of provider knowledge without which the quality production function would be compromised (Darling-Hammond 1999; Das and others 2015; Goldhaber and Brewer 1996). However, what providers are capable of doing—measured through applied knowledge or competence—is oftentimes not predictive of what they actually do in practice—denoting their level of exerted effort or performance (Das and others 2015; Hanushek and Luque 2003; Hanushek and Rivkin 2006; Kane, Rockoff, and Staiger 2008; Rethans and others 1991). Traversing the chasm between what providers know and what they actually do—or the "know-do gap"—is of paramount importance to meet quality standards in the delivery of social services and to impact human development outcomes. Service providers must work to their knowledge frontiers and consistently meet their professional duties and responsibilities. In short, finding ways to increase *provider effort* is critical to the quality of service delivery in both the education and health sectors (Das and Hammer 2014; Donabedian 1988; RAND 2012).

Accountability and Provider Effort

The notion of accountability rests on a relationship in which one party is answerable to another and is liable for his or her actions. In the realm of service delivery, this implies that a doctor or teacher feels an obligation to provide good-quality services and, at a minimum, fulfills the terms of an explicit or implicit set of commitments to the patient or student. Furthermore, the provider is prepared to take responsibility for her actions. Accountable providers are more likely to exert the effort required to carry out their duties effectively, increasing the quality of services delivered (Andrabi, Das, and Khwaja 2014; Björkman and Svensson 2009; Hastings and Weinstein 2008; Pandey, Goyal, and Sundararaman 2009; Pradhan and others 2014).[1]

A sense of accountability among providers does not always occur naturally. Rather, it can and more often than not, needs to be promoted through a variety of mechanisms (Banerjee and Duflo 2006; Chaudhury and others 2006). On the basis of a two-dimensional conceptualization (Schedler 1999), effective accountability requires monitoring and oversight mechanisms that allow one to find facts and generate evidence of actual performance and to prevent eventual underperformance or high performance from going unnoticed. It also necessitates mechanisms of enforcement that align incentives to ensure that good performance is rewarded and poor performance sanctioned (Schedler 1999). These two broad types of mechanisms—monitoring and incentives—can increase the likelihood that providers will come to work, adhere to standards and guidelines, and be responsive to client needs toward the provision of good-quality services.

On its own, monitoring—or even just the knowledge that monitoring may occur—can sometimes provide sufficient motivation for teachers, doctors, and other staff members to fulfill their professional obligations (Panagopoulos 2010). Monitoring arrangements can be formal or informal and can take place at multiple levels—by superiors within the facility, community members, or local officials. In the absence of consequences, however, monitoring may not induce behavioral changes. Monitoring is more likely to be effective when coupled with incentives, which can be negative or positive (Willis-Shattuck and others 2008; World Bank 2004). Sanctions in response to failures to carry out professional duties or rewards for good performance provide one set of motivations, for which monitoring is a prerequisite. Sanctions can be financial, as in penalties such as lost wages or benefits, or nonfinancial, such as public reprimands or professional demotions. Rewards can also be financial or nonfinancial. Financial incentives, whether in terms of salary or allowances, play a clear role in motivating providers to carry out their duties and remain in their posts. As elaborated in subsequent chapters, though, a growing body of research attests to the critical—and sometimes even more important—role of nonfinancial incentives in shaping provider effort (Ashraf, Bandiera, and Jack 2014; Francois and Vlassopoulos 2008; Mathauer and Imhoff 2006; Willis-Shattuck and others 2008). These include a broad array of incentives such as official recognition for a job well executed or the availability of continuing education and training programs that are tied to good performance. Managerial techniques—such as providing continuous feedback on staff performance, encouraging new ideas or initiatives, or involving staff in critical decisions that may affect them—can also motivate providers by fostering a positive work environment and enabling professional staff to gain recognition from their superiors, colleagues, peer groups, or communities (Dieleman, Gerretsen, and van der Wilt 2009; Harris, Cortvriend, and Hyde 2007).

Effectively monitoring provider performance is essential for enforcing all forms of incentives—whether negative or positive, financial or nonfinancial—to increase provider effort. To allocate financial and nonfinancial incentives, local health and education officials, managers, and other decision makers must have ways to evaluate staff members. Researchers and policy makers have tested a wide variety of policies, institutional arrangements, and management tools to improve the accountability of service delivery and increase the likelihood that service providers show up for work and adhere to established standards of good practice. These efforts can be classified as top-down, bottom-up, or within-facility approaches.[2]

Top-Down Accountability

As the name implies, top-down accountability aims at promoting provider effort through government oversight. Within the public sector, it includes formal administrative jurisdictions at the national, provincial, district, municipal, village or local levels, and involves agencies engaged in the provision of services or those charged with the financing or regulation of service providers, whether public or private. Government supervision and regulation of service facilities and their personnel often entail a compact, or an explicit or implicit agreement between the state and providers, to induce doctors or teachers to meet their obligations, usually in return for performance-based rewards or penalties (World Bank 2004).

Tools associated with top-down accountability entail official oversight over the performance and output of service facilities, usually by local government officials who then report up to superiors. For example, electronic methods used by local officials to monitor providers' attendance, such as through smartphones or other devices, have been shown to increase staff attendance (Banerjee and Duflo 2006; Callen and others 2013; Dhaliwal and Hanna 2014). Attaching incentives to monitoring mechanisms, such as through performance-based pay schemes, bonuses, promotions, and official recognition by local governments, have proven to induce greater commitment and compliance with standards (Banerjee, Glennerster, and Duflo 2008; Chimhutu, Lindkvist, and Lange 2014; de Walque and others 2015; Gertler and Vermeersch 2013; Huillery and Seban 2014; Muralidharan and Sundararaman 2011).

Top-down accountability faces challenges, however. In many developing countries, democracies and nondemocracies alike, the state's regulatory capacity is lacking. Even the most well-intentioned government officials may not be able to induce social service providers to fulfill their obligations either because they lack sufficient information on performance or because they have insufficient means to enforce the terms of a compact. As a result, doctors or teachers may fail to show up to work, underperform in their jobs, mistreat or neglect patients and students, or solicit bribes before they will carry out their basic duties.

Bottom-Up Accountability

Given the potential limitations of top-down accountability, bottom-up accountability gives citizens the means to directly hold providers accountable (World Bank 2004).

Patients, students, and their families are well placed to monitor their providers since they have the most direct contact with doctors, teachers, or other professional staff at their local service facilities. Methods of boosting bottom-up accountability generally rely on formal and informal means of exercising citizen or community influence over their providers. For example, community recognition of good providers that respond to the natural human desire to achieve favorable acknowledgment is a powerful source of motivation and is a relatively low-cost, informal means of inducing improved provider effort (Björkman and Svensson 2009; Panagopoulos 2010). More formal, institutionalized forms of client power are also an option. Local management of facilities, such as through school-based management or health committees composed of community members, introduces a hands-on method of monitoring provider behavior and influencing the operations of schools or health centers. Similarly, community control over budgeting for social expenditures, such as through block grant programs that empower local residents to decide on spending priorities, potentially induce providers to increase their effort to gain more resources (Olken, Onishi, and Wong 2012).

The potential negative repercussions of poor performance can shape provider behavior. The threat of exit by introducing a choice of providers may incentivize teachers or health center staff to exhibit greater effort and improve human development outcomes. For example, Couch, Shughart, and Williams (1993) find that competition from private schools leads to better test scores in the United States. In the case of healthcare, Bloom and others (2015) find that opening a new hospital in districts in England increases management performance in existing hospitals. Similarly, greater control over hiring and firing by facility-based committees can reduce provider absenteeism and increase commitment to professional duties (Duflo, Dupas, and Kremer 2015; King and Ozler 2005).

Bottom-up accountability, too, has serious limitations. First, collective action is often hard to achieve among disparate groups of citizens, unless preestablished social or personal ties have already brought them together (Lieberman 2003; Singh 2010; Tsai 2007). Second, even when these disparate groups are able to overcome collective action problems and organize, they often lack sufficient technical knowledge about social service sectors, giving them an informational disadvantage in the provider-client relationship (see Akerlof 1970, cited in Das and Hammer 2014). Third, ordinary citizens—rather than political and economic elites—often lack influence over decision makers and officials, limiting their ability to affect change in the behavior of local providers (Blimpo and Evans 2011; Patrinos, Barrera-Osorio, and Fasih 2009; Pradhan and others 2014). Lastly, even if all of these obstacles can be overcome, initiatives designed to encourage greater citizen participation and control over the allocation of resources are subject to elite capture, limiting the efficacy of citizen voice in promoting provider effort (Dasgupta and Beard 2007; Platteau 2000).

Within-Facility Accountability
Within the accountability framework, one aspect has been underemphasized, notably the role of supervisors in the facilities at the frontlines of service delivery.

The way in which accountability is promoted and ensured within schools and health centers is critical to inducing compliance with technical and professional standards and other measures of provider effort, which in turn can improve the quality of health and education service provision. Thus, mechanisms of promoting provider effort within facilities deserve more attention than they have received thus far in development research as they may be able to address some of the limitations of both top-down and bottom-up accountability mechanisms.

An emphasis on within-facility accountability capitalizes on the technical knowledge of supervisors within health centers and schools and on the proximity to the actual service delivery exchange between providers and clients. These advantages address two issues that may bedevil efforts to build accountability in service delivery, notably the "observability challenge" and the "farther outcome problem."

The Observability Challenge

The observability challenge refers to the inherent difficulty in observing and evaluating what doctors and teachers actually do in their workplaces and especially in clinical examination rooms and classrooms. Monitoring requires that supervisors have sufficient technical knowledge to distinguish between different levels and types of provider effort, as well as proximity to observe these periodically. As trained physicians, chief medical officers (CMOs) have the background to assess whether doctors follow proper protocols or prescribe the correct treatment plan. Similarly, principals are qualified to determine whether teachers provide adequate instructional support to students, which requires knowledge of the principles of pedagogy and instructional evaluation. CMOs and school principals are located within facilities, have the mandate to observe the performance of their employees, and possess the technical know-how to interpret what they see. The combination of these attributes therefore gives these facility-level managers unique advantages in fulfilling the monitoring function of accountability.

The Farther Outcome Problem

The farther outcome problem refers to the use of outcomes that are more easily observed and quantified, such as health outcomes or student test scores, to gauge and incentivize provider effort, rather than what actually occurs in clinical examination rooms and classrooms. But the use of such indicators may not be effective in improving the quality of services for two reasons. First, many factors that influence easily observed and quantifiable outcomes are outside the control of providers. Individual, family, and contextual characteristics all influence students' test scores and patients' health outcomes, making it challenging to attribute changes in these outcomes to service providers' actions. Second, relying on easily observable and quantified outcomes creates incentives that may not promote optimal provider behavior. In the education sector, reliance on test scores as performance assessment criteria can incentivize teachers to "teach to the test" or invest more in test preparation while neglecting actual student learning. In the case of healthcare, reliance on farther outcomes such as patient surveys may incentivize providers to prescribe medications that are not necessary to satisfy patients who lack the knowledge to accurately evaluate provider performance (Das and Hammer 2014). A focus on within-facility assessments of teacher effort can help overcome this problem. Because they are often trained as teachers and have spent numerous years teaching in the classroom before entering school administration, school principals can detect and assess different dimensions of teacher effort when they see them. Similarly, CMOs have the technical knowledge to rely on more proximate measures of effort that can be generated within facilities by reviewing medical records, observing clinical interactions, or employing other methods.

Essentially, within-facility accountability may be able to overcome the observability challenge and the farther outcome problem because it relies on supervisors who are proximate to and knowledgeable of client/provider interactions. Key tools to promote within-facility accountability entail systems to monitor and incentivize greater provider effort (Dieleman, Gerretsen, and van der Wilt 2009; Harris, Cortvriend, and Hyde 2007; Kabene and others 2006; West and others 2006). Monitoring can involve random checks of medical records or verification of teachers' lesson plans. It may also involve joining health providers in clinics or conducting classroom observations. Other tools may incorporate the use of surveys to gauge client satisfaction or systems to track provider absenteeism at the facility. Within health centers and schools, managers can institutionalize a variety of positive and negative incentives to encourage doctors or teachers to apply their knowledge and training in clinical interactions or in the classroom, thereby exerting high levels of effort. Positive incentives might include financial rewards and bonuses, if budgets permit. They might also entail nonfinancial approaches, such as fostering workplace satisfaction by building a team-oriented culture, granting staff members greater autonomy in their daily responsibilities, or recognizing staff through "employee-of-the-month" awards and related approaches. Examples of negative incentives are official reprimands and sanctions, the withholding of salaries or imposition of financial penalties, or, at the extreme, the suspension or termination of employment. Research on human resource management indicates that positive incentives are more likely to induce greater provider effort than sanctions, which can backfire by reducing workplace morale (Ashraf, Bandiera, and Jack 2014; Mathauer and Imhoff 2006; Willis-Shattuck and others 2008).

Within-facility accountability does not operate in a vacuum and therefore cannot be entirely divorced from top-down and bottom-up forms of accountability. The engagement of local authorities and the broader community may compel CMOs or school principals to monitor more rigorously and to design and implement programs that elicit greater commitment to professional responsibilities. Indeed, the very fact that the efficacy of a given monitoring or incentive scheme varies across different studies suggests that the context in which implementation occurs moderates its impact (Pritchett and Sandefur 2013). The involvement of local authorities, communities, and management, adaptation to local circumstances, and the active involvement of local staff to identify and implement solutions to problems increase the success of policies aimed at better performance of service facilities in low- and middle-income countries (Christenson and Cleary 1990;

Dieleman, Gerretsen, and van der Wilt 2009; Johnson, Monk, and Swain 2000). Thus, the full value of within-facility accountability may be best realized when it works in coordination with top-down and bottom-up forms of accountability.

Motivation of the Present Report

Ultimately, doctors, teachers, and other staff members who perform well and devote themselves to fulfilling their duties are accountable providers. The key challenge, then, is to seek effective ways to boost provider accountability. A combination of distinct mechanisms—monitoring and incentives—is likely to yield the most marked improvements in provider performance. These mechanisms can operate at multiple levels through top-down, bottom-up, and within-facility accountability.[3]

Research on accountability and quality of services has thus far underemphasized within-facility accountability—the focus of this report. Compelling reasons exist to devote further policy attention to this node in the service delivery chain. The managers of service institutions (for example, CMOs and school principals) are uniquely well situated and qualified to monitor and incentivize higher provider effort given their technical skills, experience, and proximity to the service delivery exchange. Furthermore, to the extent that they entail minimal expense and work with existing human capital, policies to promote within-facility accountability through monitoring and incentives can be cost-effective and feasible. Given that service delivery institutions are located at the nexus of local government offices and communities, within-facility accountability is also affected by external influences, whether from state agencies, civil society organizations, or citizens themselves. Ultimately, the way in which accountability is promoted and ensured within health centers and schools determines how effective these measures will be in increasing provider effort.

This report investigates the linkages between within-facility accountability and provider effort in the health and education sectors in Jordan through an original study in primary healthcare facilities and rigorous analyses of existing data on the education sector in Jordan. The limited contributions of the structural dimensions of quality to human development outcomes and the extensive resources that Jordan has already invested in its health and educational systems, which are not likely to yield substantial additional payoffs, justify this focus. Indeed, Jordan's social expenditures are relatively high vis-à-vis other countries in the region, with average public expenditures on health and education accounting for between 7 and 8 percent of gross domestic product (GDP) in the past three decades, whereas governments in other Middle East and North Africa (MENA) countries outside of the oil-rich Gulf countries spent between 5.4 and 6.4 percent of GDP on the social sectors in the same period (Cammett and others 2015). In comparison with other middle-income countries, Jordan also exhibits high social expenditures. For example, between 1996 and 2013, average public spending on health as a percentage of GDP was about twice as high in Jordan as in the average middle-income country. Such high levels of spending do not necessarily buy superior health outcomes: in 2013, public expenditure on health was 3 percent of GDP in Jordan and only 1.4 percent in Sri Lanka, yet the infant mortality rate was 16.3 per 1,000 and life expectancy at birth was 73.9 years in the former country while the infant mortality rate was 8.7 per 1,000 and life expectancy was 74.2 in the latter, despite Sri Lanka's low per capita GDP (World Bank 2015). The gap between expenditures and outcomes is especially evident in the education sector. Enrollment rates in Jordan are high, but the performance of 15-year-old Jordanians on international assessments reveals that it is one of the lowest scoring countries participating in the Program for International Student Assessment (PISA) exam (OECD 2012). At the same time, public expenditure on education as a percentage of GDP was 3.4 percent in 2011, below the Organisation for Economic Co-operation and Development (OECD) average of 5.2 percent but on par with levels in countries that performed much more strongly in international assessment, such as Singapore, Japan, and Hong Kong (OECD 2012; World Bank 2012). The failure of structural investment to substantially improve outcomes in Jordan appears to also hold in the broader MENA region. Analysis of the health and education sectors in Jordan thus provides a valuable case study for understanding provider service in the entire region.[4] Finding ways to encourage doctors and teachers to fulfill their professional duties and work to their knowledge frontiers promises to yield tangible improvements while entailing minimal additional financial outlays.

Report Roadmap

Chapter 2 describes the role of accountability in promoting teacher effort and student learning and provides a brief overview of the Jordanian education sector. The chapter then presents the design, methods, and results of a rigorous empirical study linking accountability mechanisms used by school principals to teacher effort and student outcomes in Jordan. Chapter 3 first focuses on the role of accountability in improving the delivery of healthcare in the Jordanian health sector and describes the design, methods, and results of an original research study on the relationship between accountability mechanisms used by CMOs and health provider effort in Jordan. Chapter 4 builds on the lessons of these original research studies to elaborate a series of policy recommendations aimed at capitalizing on within-facility accountability to improve provider effort and, ultimately, human development outcomes in Jordan.

Notes

1. Kosack and Fung (2014) present a framework to explain the conditions that shape the effectiveness of interventions to improve provider accountability.
2. This classification is aligned with the accountability relationship framework described in the 2004 World Development Report, *Making Services Work for the Poor* (World Bank 2004).
3. Such mechanisms have been reflected upon in the MENA Flagship Report "Trust, Voice, and Incentives: Learning from Local Success Stories in the Middle East and

North Africa" (Brixi, Lust, and Woolcock 2015), which examined the role of trust, incentives, and citizen engagement as critical determinants of service delivery performance in both the health and education sectors in MENA countries. Examining the powerful role of bottom-up accountability mechanisms, the report incorporated two case studies from Jordan (one in health and another in the education sector) where communities have managed to attain extraordinary outcomes using innovative local solutions to the prevailing problems. The present study builds on this previous endeavor by expounding on the accountability mechanisms within service delivery facilities.

4. In the broader MENA region, health and education expenditures as a percentage of GDP were cut minimally or remained stable during periods of fiscal austerity while rank averages of the Human Development Index declined markedly from the 1990s through the 2010s (Cammett and others 2015). The MENA region devoted a higher percentage of GDP to health during the 1990s than East Asia yet had significantly lower health outcomes (World Bank 2002). Literacy is also lower than expected given income levels. In 2010, adult literacy in the developing countries of the MENA region was 77.9 percent, as compared with 81.4 percent in low- and middle-income countries and 98.3 percent in OECD countries (World Development Indicators). Indicators of academic performance, such as the Trends in International Mathematics and Science Study (TIMSS), which measures fourth- and eighth-grade student outcomes and is administered every four years internationally to a large sample of countries, as well as the PISA of the OECD, indicate that students in the region fare poorly in comparison with students in countries with similar per capita income levels (TIMSS 2007).

References

Akerlof, George A. 1970. "The Market for 'Lemons': Quality Uncertainty and the Market Mechanism." *Quarterly Journal of Economics* 84 (3): 488–500.

Andrabi, Tahir, Jishnu Das, and Asim Ijaz Khwaja. 2014. *Report Cards: The Impact of Providing School and Child Test Scores on Educational Markets.* Cambridge, MA: Harvard University Press.

Ashraf, Nava, Oriana Bandiera, and B. Kelsey Jack. 2014. "No Margin, No Mission? A Field Experiment on Incentives for Public Service Delivery." *Journal of Public Economics* 120: 1–17.

Banerjee, Abhijit, and Esther Duflo. 2006. "Addressing Absence." *Journal of Economic Perspectives* 20 (1): 117–32.

Banerjee, Abhijit V., Esther Duflo, and Rachel Glennerster. 2008. "Putting a Band-Aid on a Corpse: Incentives for Nurses in the Indian Public Health Care System." *Journal of the European Economic Association* 6 (2–3): 487–500.

Björkman, Martina, and Jakob Svensson. 2009. "Power to the People: Evidence from a Randomized Field Experiment of a Community-Based Monitoring Project in Uganda." *Quarterly Journal of Economics* 124 (2): 735–69.

Blimpo, Moussa P., and David K. Evans. 2011. "School-Based Management and Educational Outcomes: Lessons from a Randomized Field Experiment." Working Paper, World Bank, Washington, DC.

Bloom, Nicholas, Carol Propper, Stephan Seiler, and John van Reenen. 2015. "The Impact of Competition on Management Quality: Evidence from Public Hospitals." *The Review of Economic Studies* 82 (2): 457–89.

Brixi, Hana, Erin Lust, and Michael Woolcock. 2015. Trust, Voice, and Incentives: Learning from Local Success Stories in Service Delivery in the Middle East and North Africa. Washington, DC: World Bank.

Callen, Michael Joseph, Saad Gulzar, Syed Ali Hasanain, and Muhammad Yasir Khan. 2013. "The Political Economy of Public Employee Absence: Experimental Evidence from Pakistan." SSRN Working Paper 2316245, Social Science Research Network, Rochester, NY. https://papers.ssrn.com/sol3/papers2.cfm?abstract _id=2316245.

Cammett, Melani, Ishac Diwan, Alan Richards, and John Waterbury. 2015. *A Political Economy of the Middle East.* 4th ed. Boulder, CO: Westview.

Chaudhury, N., J. Hammer, M. Kremer, K. Muralidharan, and F. H. Rogers. 2006. "Missing in Action: Teacher and Health Worker Absence in Developing Countries." *Journal of Economic Perspectives* 20 (1): 91–116.

Chimhutu, Victor, Ida Lindkvist, and Siri Lange. 2014. "When Incentives Work Too Well: Locally Implemented Pay for Performance (P4P) and Adverse Sanctions towards Home Birth in Tanzania—A Qualitative Study." *BMC Health Services Research* 14 (1): 23.

Christenson, Sandra L., and Maureen Cleary. 1990. "Consultation and the Parent-Educator Partnership: A Perspective. *Journal of Educational and Psychological Consultation* 1 (3): 219–41.

Das, Jishnu, Alaka Holla, Aakash Mohpal, and Karthik Muralidharan. 2015. "Quality and Accountability in Healthcare Delivery: Audit Evidence from Primary Care Providers in India." Policy Research Working Paper 7334, World Bank.

Cristia, J., P. Ibarrán, S. Cueto, A. Santiago, and E. Severín. 2012. "Technology and Child Development: Evidence from the One Laptop per Child Program." IZA Discussion Paper 6401, Forschungsinstitut zur Zukunft der Arbeit GmbH, Bonn, Germany.

Couch, Jim F., William F. Shughart, and Al L. Williams. 1993. "Private School Enrollment and Public School Performance." *Public Choice* 76 (4): 301–12.

Darling-Hammond, Linda. 1999. "Target Time toward Teachers." *Journal of Staff Development* 20 (2): 31–36.

Das, Jishnu, and Jeffrey Hammer. 2014. "Quality of Primary Care in Low-Income Countries: Facts and Economics." *Annual Review of Economics* 6: 525–53.

Das, Jishnu, Alaka Holla, Aakash Mohpal, and Karthik Muralidharan. 2015. "Quality and Accountability in Healthcare Delivery: Audit Evidence from Primary Care Providers in India." Policy Research Working Paper 7334, World Bank, Washington, DC.

Dasgupta, Aniruddha, and Victoria A. Beard. 2007. "Community Driven Development, Collective Action and Elite Capture in Indonesia." *Development and Change* 38 (2): 229–49.

de Walque, Damien, Paul J. Gertler, Sergio Bautista-Arredondo, Ada Kwan, Christel Vermeersch, Jean de Dieu Bizimana, Agnès Binagwaho, and Jeanine Condo. 2015. "Using Provider Performance Incentives to Increase HIV Testing and Counseling Services in Rwanda." *Journal of Health Economics* 40: 1–9.

Dhaliwal, Iqbal, and Rema Hanna. 2014. "Deal with the Devil: The Successes and Limitations of Bureaucratic Reform in India." NBER Working Paper 201482, National Bureau of Economic Research, Cambridge, MA.

Dieleman, Marjolein, Barend Gerretsen, and Gert Jan van der Wilt. 2009. "Human Resource Management Interventions to Improve Health Workers' Performance in Low- and Middle-Income Countries: A Realist Review." *Health Research Policy and Systems* 7 (7): 1–13.

Donabedian, Avedis. 1988. "The Quality of Care: How Can It Be Assessed?" *Journal of the American Medical Association* 260 (12): 1743–48.

Duflo, Esther, Pascaline Dupas, and Michael Kremer. 2015. "School Governance, Teacher Incentives, and Pupil–Teacher Ratios: Experimental Evidence from Kenyan Primary Schools." *Journal of Public Economics* 123: 92–110.

Francois, Patrick, and Michael Vlassopoulos. 2008. "Pro-social Motivation and the Delivery of Social Services." *CESifo Economic Studies* 54 (1): 22–54.

Gertler, Paul, and Christel Vermeersch. 2013. "Using Performance Incentives to Improve Medical Care Productivity and Health Outcomes." NBER Working Paper 19046, National Bureau of Economic Research, Cambridge, MA.

Glewwe, Paul, Eric A. Hanushek, Sarah Humpage, and Renato Ravina. 2013. "School Resources and Educational Outcomes in Developing Countries: A Review of the Literature from 1990 to 2010." In *Education Policy in Developing Countries*, edited by Paul Glewwe. Chicago: University of Chicago Press.

Glewwe, Paul, Michael Kremer, Sylvie Moulin, and Eric Zitzewitz. 2004. "Retrospective vs. Prospective Analyses of School Inputs: The Case of Flip Charts in Kenya." *Journal of Development Economics* 74 (1): 251–68.

Goldhaber, Dan D., and Dominic J. Brewer. 1996. "Evaluating the Effect of Teacher Degree Level on Educational Performance." Evaluative Report, Westat, Rockville, MD. http://files.eric.ed.gov/fulltext/ED406400.pdf.

Hanushek, Eric A. 2003. "The Failure of Input-Based Schooling Policies." *The Economic Journal* 113 (485): F64–98.

———. and Javier A. Luque. 2003. "Efficiency and Equity in Schools Around the World." *Economics of Education Review* 22 (5): 481–502.

Hanushek, Eric A., and Steven G. Rivkin. 2006. "Teacher Quality." *Handbook of the Economics of Education* 2: 1051–78.

Harris, Claire, Penny Cortvriend, and Paula Hyde. 2007. "Human Resource Management and Performance in Healthcare Organisations." *Journal of Health Organization and Management* 21 (4–5): 448–59.

Hastings, Justine S., and Jeffrey M. Weinstein. 2008. "Information, School Choice, and Academic Achievement: Evidence from Two Experiments." *Quarterly Journal of Economics* 123 (4): 1373–414.

Huillery, Elise, and Juliette Seban. 2014. "Performance-Based Financing, Motivation and Final Output in the Health Sector: Experimental Evidence from the Democratic Republic of Congo." No. 2014–12, Sciences Po Economics Discussion Papers, Department of Economics, Paris.

Johnson, Sally, Martin Monk, and Julian Swain. 2000. "Constraints on Development and Change to Science Teachers' Practice in Egyptian Classrooms." *Journal of Education for Teaching: International Research and Pedagogy* 26 (1): 9–24.

Kabene, Stefane M., Carole Orchard, John M. Howard, Mark A. Soriano, and Raymond Leduc. 2006. "The Importance of Human Resources Management in Health Care: A Global Context." *Human Resources for Health* 4 (20): 1–17.

Kane, Thomas J., Jonah E. Rockoff, and Douglas O. Staiger. 2008. "What Does Certification Tell Us about Teacher Effectiveness? Evidence from New York City." *Economics of Education Review* 27 (6): 615–31.

King, Elizabeth M., and Berk Ozler. 2005. "What's Decentralization Got to Do with Learning? School Autonomy and Student Performance." Discussion Paper 54:51–60, Interfaces for Advanced Economic Analysis, Kyoto University.

Kosack, Stephen, and Archon Fung. 2014. "Does Transparency Improve Governance?" *Annual Review of Political Science* 17: 65–87.

Lieberman, Evan. 2003. *Race and Regionalism in the Politics of Taxation in Brazil and South Africa.* Cambridge, UK: Cambridge University Press.

Mathauer, Inke, and Ingo Imhoff. 2006. "Health Worker Motivation in Africa: The Role of Non-financial Incentives and Human Resource Management Tools." *Human Resources for Health* 4 (1): 1–17.

Mitchell, Pamela H., Sandra Ferketich, and Bonnie M. Jennings. 1998. "Quality Health Outcomes Model." *Image: The Journal of Nursing Scholarship* 30 (1): 43–46.

Muralidharan, Karthik, and Venkatesh Sundararaman. 2011. "Teacher Performance Pay: Experimental Evidence from India." *Journal of Political Economy* 119 (1): 39–77.

OECD (Organisation for Economic Co-operation and Development). 2012. "Program for International Student Assessment 2012." OECD, Paris.

Olken, Benjamin A., Junko Onishi, and Susan Wong. 2012. "Should Aid Reward Performance? Evidence from a Field Experiment on Health and Education in Indonesia." NBER Working Paper, National Bureau of Economic Research, Cambridge, MA.

Panagopoulos, Costas. 2010. "Affect, Social Pressure and Prosocial Motivation: Field Experimental Evidence of the Mobilizing Effects of Pride, Shame and Publicizing Voting Behavior." *Political Behavior* 32 (3): 369–86.

Pandey, Priyanka, Sangeeta Goyal, and Venkatesh Sundararaman. 2009. "Community Participation in Public Schools: Impact of Information Campaigns in Three Indian States." *Education Economics* 17 (3): 355–75.

Patrinos, Harry Anthony, Felipe Barrera-Osorio, and Tazeen Fasih. 2009. *Decentralized Decision-Making in Schools: The Theory and Evidence on School-Based Management.* Washington, DC: World Bank.

Platteau, Jean-Philippe. 2000. *Institutions, Social Norms, and Economic Development.* Amsterdam: Harwood Academic Publishers.

Pradhan, Menno, Daniel Suryadarma, Amanda Beatty, Maisy Wong, Arya Gaduh, Armida Alisjahbana, and Rima Prama Artha. 2014. "Improving Educational Quality through Enhancing Community Participation: Results from a Randomized Field Experiment in Indonesia." *American Economic Journal: Applied Economics* 6 (2): 105–26.

Pritchett, Lant, and Justin Sandefur. 2013. "Context Matters for Size: Why External Validity Claims and Development Practice Do Not Mix." *Journal of Globalization and Development* 4 (2): 161–97.

RAND. 2012. *Teachers Matter: Understanding Teachers' Impact on Student Achievement.* Santa Monica, CA: RAND Corporation.

Rethans, Jan-Joost, Ferd Sturmans, Riet Drop, Cees van der Vleuten, and Pie Hobus. "Does Competence of General Practitioners Predict Their Performance? Comparison between Examination Setting and Actual Practice." *British Medical Journal* 303 (6814): 1377–80.

Roberts, M. J., W. C. Hsiao, P. Berman, and M. R. Reich. 2008. *Getting Health Reform Right: A Guide to Improving Performance and Equity*. New York: Oxford University Press.

Schedler, Andreas. 1999. "Conceptualizing Accountability." In *The Self-Restraining State: Power and Accountability in New Democracies*, edited by Andreas Schedler, Larry Diamond and Marc F. Plattner, 13–28. Boulder, CO: Lynne Rienner Publishers.

Singh, Prerna. 2010. "We-Ness and Welfare: A Longitudinal Analysis of Social Development in Kerala, India." *World Development* 39 (2): 282–93.

TIMSS (Trends in International Mathematics and Science Study). 2007. *Assessment: International Association for the Evaluation of Educational Achievement (IEA)*. TIMSS & PIRLS International Study Center, Lynch School of Education, Boston College.

Tsai, Lily. 2007. *Accountability without Democracy: Solidary Groups and Public Goods Provision in Rural China*. Cambridge, UK: Cambridge University Press.

West, Michael A., James P. Guthrie, Jeremy F. Dawson, Carol S. Borrill, and Matthew Carter. 2006. "Reducing Patient Mortality in Hospitals: The Role of Human Resource Management." *Journal of Organizational Behavior* 27 (7): 983–1002.

Willis-Shattuck, Mischa, Posy Bidwell, Steve Thomas, Laura Wyness, Duane Blaauw, and Prudence Ditlopo. 2008. "Motivation and Retention of Health Workers in Developing Countries: A Systematic Review." *BMC Health Services Research* 8 (1): 1–8.

World Bank. 2002. *Reducing Vulnerability and Increasing Opportunity: Social Protection in the Middle East and North Africa*. Washington, DC: World Bank.

———. 2003. *Better Governance for Development in the Middle East and North Africa: Enhancing Inclusiveness and Accountability*. Washington, DC: World Bank.

———. 2004. *World Development Report 2004: Making Services Work for the Poor*. Washington, DC: World Bank.

———. 2012. World Development Indicators. http://data.worldbank.org/data-catalog /world-development-indicators.

———. 2015. *World Development Indicators 2015*. Washington, DC: World Bank.

CHAPTER 2

Education Quality, Teacher Effort, and Accountability

Introduction

To improve student learning, researchers and policy makers have strived to better understand the different school factors involved in the education process and to estimate their relative contribution to student learning. These factors include school infrastructure and facilities, classroom supplies, learning materials, the curricula, class size, the school principal, and the teacher, and can be thought of in terms of inputs within the school education production function.

In the last decade, an increasing number of rigorous impact evaluations have been conducted to test the individual contribution of many of these inputs to student learning. From supplying instructional flip charts in Kenya (Glewwe and others 2004), to reducing class sizes in the United States (Krueger 1999; Krueger and Whitmore 2001), Bolivia (Urquiola 2006), Israel (Angrist and Lavy 1999), and India (Banerjee and others 2007), to equipping schools and students with computers in Peru (Cristia and others 2012) and Colombia (Barrera-Osorio and Linden 2009), the evidence consistently suggests that these inputs have small effects on student learning—if at all.

The evidence also points to the fact that among all school inputs, teachers are what matter the most. In fact, a teacher is estimated to have two to three times the impact of any other school factor on student learning (RAND 2012). Effect sizes attributed to a one standard deviation (SD) increase in teacher quality range from 0.08 SD for reading and 0.11 SD for math (Kane and Staiger 2008) to as high as 0.26 SD and 0.36 SD for reading and math, respectively (Nye, Spyros, and Hedges 2004). In other words, when using the more conservative estimates, moving a student from a teacher in the 5th percentile of teacher quality to the 95th percentile in the United States increases student outcomes by roughly 0.33 SD. In developing countries, the impact of teacher quality is even larger, with a similar move yielding a 0.85 SD increase in student outcomes (Bau and Das, 2016). The magnitude of such an effect becomes evident when compared to the effect sizes associated with a full academic year of instruction of roughly a 0.25 SD increase in test scores (Kane 2004), and typical measures of income achievement gaps of 0.7–1 SD (Hanushek and Rivkin 2010). The effects are even more dramatic when considering that a series of high- or low-quality teachers throughout school years compounds these effects and can lead to unbridgeable gaps in student learning levels (Bruns and Luque 2014).

With teacher quality the single most effective school input to improve or undermine student learning, a key priority for policy makers and school administrators is to identify the drivers of teacher quality and find ways in which they can be boosted. Contrary to common belief, a recent strand of the education literature has found that high-quality teachers cannot be reliably identified based on easily observable characteristics such as their level of education, certification status, or years of experience—important determinants of teacher pay in many countries. With regard to teachers' level of education, the evidence suggests that having, for example, a master's degree in the United States, or a university degree in over 30 developing countries studied, has no systematic relationship with teacher quality as measured by student outcomes. Moreover, there is little indication that specialized training (in addition to or in place of a university degree) has any impact on student learning (Hanushek and Luque 2003; Hanushek and Rivkin 2006). The picture is no different for teacher certification. A study conducted in New York City public schools found that, on average, the certification status of a teacher (certified, uncertified, or alternatively certified) has at most small impacts on student test scores (Kane, Rockoff, and Staiger 2006). As for teachers' years of experience in the profession, the literature in developed and developing countries alike indicates that teacher experience improves quality in the early years (1–2 years) of teaching; however, increased experience beyond this has no effect on teacher quality (Bau and Das, 2016; Hanushek and others 2005). In summary, these observable characteristics together explain no more than 5 percent of the variation in teacher quality (Bau and Das, 2016).

One explanation is that some teachers do not perform up to their knowledge frontier. Arguably, teachers' education and years of experience, in addition to other inherent characteristics such as their talent, shape the higher bound of their knowledge or ability to translate a given level of school-related inputs (for example, the curricula, classroom supplies, learning materials) into learning for their students. What teachers know, however, might not be consistently reflected in what they actually do in the classroom. This "know-do" gap might be a key explanatory factor of the large and persistent differences in teacher quality among those teachers with the same level of education and/or years of experience. In other words, at any given level of education and/or experience, teachers might exert different levels of effort in their classrooms. As such, with the largest share of countries' education expenditure devoted to teachers (in the form of salaries), the know-do gap may be one of the most significant sources of inefficiency in the education system. At the same time, closing this gap by increasing teachers' effort up to their knowledge frontier may be likely to have a very significant impact on student learning.

Teacher Effort

In its most elementary level, low teacher effort can take the form of teacher absenteeism. It is reasonable to assume that teachers know that their timely attendance to class is needed for their students to learn. Yet teacher absenteeism is a significant problem in many countries. Using unannounced visits, nationally representative surveys found that 16 percent of teachers in Bangladesh, 14 percent in Ecuador, 25 percent in India, 19 percent in Indonesia, 11 percent in Peru, and 27 percent in Uganda were absent during normal school hours (Chaudhury and others 2005). As expected, closing this very elementary know-do gap by increasing teacher effort yields significant effects on student learning. For example, evidence from a randomized controlled trial in rural India shows that reducing teacher absenteeism from 42 percent to 21 percent increases student test scores by 0.17 SD (Duflo, Hanna, and Ryan 2012).

But even when teachers do show up to work, low effort can persist in teachers' choice of classroom time allocation. Teachers' classroom time can be thought of in terms of three sets of activities with descending levels of effort: instructional activities, classroom management activities (for example, taking attendance, cleaning the blackboard, or distributing papers), and time spent completely off-task by being absent from the room or engaging in non-instructional socializing activities (Stallings 1986). Although it is reasonable to assume that teachers know that good practice for classroom time use consists of maximizing instructional time, minimizing classroom management activities, and abstaining from off-task activities, evidence from a number of developing countries suggests large variations in teachers' use of classroom time across schools, which in turn is strongly predictive of student achievement. The single most consistent finding across a sample of schools in Rio de Janeiro, Mexico City, Honduras, Colombia, Jamaica, and Peru is the negative association between time off-task and student achievement. For example, in Rio de Janeiro, classroom observations revealed that the top 10 percent of performing schools spent an average of 70 percent of classroom time on instruction, 27 percent in classroom management, and only 3 percent off-task. This stands in stark contrast with the bottom 10 percent of performing schools, which spent only 54 percent of classroom time on instruction and a surprisingly high share of their time on classroom management (39 percent) and off-task (7 percent), resulting in students receiving an average 32 fewer days of instruction per academic year compared with their counterparts in high-performing schools (Bruns and Luque 2014).

Yet, as these elementary levels of teacher effort become satisfied (that is, as the teacher absenteeism rate approaches zero and classroom time spent on instructional activities is nearly optimal), more substantive measures of teacher effort will be needed to understand differences in teacher quality. The case of Jordan is particularly illustrative in this matter. According to administrative data from school principal reports, Jordan benefits from an average teacher absenteeism rate of only 2.6 percent. Moreover, classroom observations suggest that, on average, teachers spend barely 4.5 percent of classroom time on non-instructional activities, and that at virtually no time are teachers observed to be outside of the classroom during their lesson (USAID 2012). Within-country variance in students' Program for International Student Assessment (PISA) math test scores, however, reveal a substantive gap between students at the 10th percentile (290 points) and their counterparts at the 90th percentile (485 points) (OECD 2012). Such variability in student outcomes may suggest important differences in teacher quality that are not captured in the elementary measures of teacher effort. Yet although less evident, low levels of more substantive measures of effort can be prevalent among teachers with excellent attendance rates who spend an optimal level of time in instructional activities.

A variety of frameworks developed to assess a teacher's classroom instructional practice could help capture more substantive measures of teacher effort. These include the Framework for Teaching (FFT) developed by Charlotte Danielson, the Classroom Assessment Scoring System (CLASS) developed at the University of Virginia, the Mathematical Quality of Instruction (MQI) developed at the University of Michigan and Harvard University, and the Protocol for Language Arts Teaching Observation (PLATO) and the Quality Science Teaching (QST), both developed at Stanford University. Broadly, these frameworks provide a set of dimensions, such as providing continuous feedback to students and designing coherent instruction, to mention a few, to assess teacher practices within the classroom. Evidence from the United States has found a correlation between these dimensions—as assessed by qualified observers—and gains in student outcomes as high as 0.18 SD (for FFT) and 0.25 SD (for CLASS). In fact, moving a teacher at the bottom quartile of the distribution on these dimensions to the top quartile corresponds to 0.06 SD and 0.08 SD in student outcome gains as measured by TFF and CLASS, respectively (Gates Foundation 2012). This suggests that teachers may be exerting suboptimal levels of effort in these substantial dimensions.

Holding Teachers Accountable to Increase Teacher Effort

Against this backdrop, increasing teacher effort is a key priority for policy makers aiming to improve student outcomes. Doing so requires holding teachers accountable through, on the one hand, monitoring mechanisms that allow one to find facts and generate evidence on what teachers actually do, and, on the other hand, mechanisms to incentivize high effort and penalize shirking. Yet monitoring efforts face a critical "observability challenge," described in the subsection below. Incentive schemes also encounter a "farther outcome problem," also explained below, making the exercise of teacher accountability quite challenging.

The Observability Challenge

Monitoring and overseeing teachers' level of effort—accountability's first function—require teacher effort to be observable. The clearest example of this is in India, where an experiment that provided cameras to teachers to take pictures of themselves with their students at the beginning and end of each class with a tamper-proof date and time function allowed decision makers to observe teachers' attendance and to make teachers' salaries a function of their attendance rate; teacher absenteeism rates decreased by 21 percentage points (Duflo, Hanna, and Ryan 2012).

Yet as elementary levels of teacher effort (such as teacher attendance) are met and more substantial measures of teacher effort become necessary to explain differences in teacher quality, efforts to bring suboptimal levels of effort up to teachers' knowledge frontier face a twofold observability challenge. On one hand, higher technical knowledge is required to distinguish between different levels of teacher effort. While assessing teachers' level of effort through their attendance rate only requires knowledge of whether or not a teacher came to school, a similar assessment based on teachers' level of instructional support to students, for example, necessitates technical knowledge of language modeling, instructional conversation, literacy instruction, richness of instructional methods, concept development, and use of formative assessments (Hamre and Pianta 2007).

On the other hand, and closely tied to the knowledge challenge, is the proximity problem. The closer the measure of teacher effort is to the heart of teaching, the harder it is to observe effort for those who are outside the classroom and school. It is feasible for school principals, students' parents, school committees, and even decision makers to observe teacher attendance. But even with the necessary technical knowledge, parents and school committees would only be able to observe teachers' level of instructional support to students if they had access to classrooms, which tends not to be the case in many countries. On the other side, with several schools to oversee, district supervisors or decision makers might be able to sporadically observe teachers' level of instructional support, but not in a systematic fashion. Arguably, with both the necessary technical knowledge and the proximity to teachers' classrooms, school principals seem to be best positioned to fulfill the monitoring function of accountability.

The Farther Outcome Problem

Recognizing the accountability void in many teacher compensation systems, some scholars and policy makers have recently begun to devise powerful incentives for teachers. As with the example of the photographic cameras in India, once decision makers were able to observe teachers' effort (that is, their attendance rate), they tied rewards and sanctions directly to this level of effort and were able to significantly reduce the absenteeism rate (Duflo, Hanna, and Ryan 2012). Yet with relatively low levels of observability for substantive measures of teacher effort to tie their incentives to, they have turned to a farther outcome they can observe: student test scores.

That providing teacher incentives will improve student test scores as teachers exert higher levels of effort seems intuitive in principle, but the evidence of its effectiveness thus far is mixed. An experiment in India that provided bonuses to teachers based on their students' test scores increased math and language scores by 0.28 SD, while also increasing the likelihood of teachers assigning homework and classwork and paying special attention to weaker students (Muralidharan and

Sundararaman 2011). In contrast, a similar experiment in Kenya that rewarded schools based on student achievement found that teachers increased test preparation sessions, which resulted in higher scores in multiple choice tests but had no effect on open-ended question tests, suggesting no actual student learning (Glewwe, Ilias, and Kremer 2010). If anything, the findings in this strand of literature have cautioned about some of the undesirable and perverse practices through which higher test scores are achieved, void of actual student learning. It is reasonable to assume that by tying incentives to students' test scores, many teachers will increase their levels of effort only in those activities that are less costly to them and that are most effective in achieving immediate student gains as measured by test scores. Veiled by the observability challenge, again, those not close enough to the classroom would fail to notice on time these undesirable, perverse practices.

The Role of School Principals

The key role that school principals can play in teacher accountability systems by easing the "farther outcome problem" and circumventing the "observability challenge" has been underemphasized thus far. Principals can play a key role in easing the farther outcome problem inherent to teacher accountability mechanisms used by policy makers ("top-down accountability") and/or school committees and parents ("bottom-up accountability"). As complements to top-down and/or bottom-up accountability, principals' monitoring and enforcement capacities within a school can be a powerful tool in ensuring that student outcomes are a product of increasing levels of effort in desirable teaching practices and, at minimum, detecting when they are not.

School principals are not constrained by the twofold observability challenge. With many of them trained as teachers and having spent numerous years teaching in the classroom before entering school administration, it is reasonable to assume that principals can identify different levels of substantive aspects of teacher effort when they see them. Furthermore, by sharing the same work space as teachers, and having the well-functioning of every classroom in the school as their main job, direct observation of teacher practices in all classrooms within a school is not only technically feasible for them, but also an implicit continuous responsibility (Bruns and Luque 2014).

Principals that leverage this position of visibility by continuously monitoring teachers to become aware of potential know-do gaps in their school's classrooms could effectively contribute to bringing teachers' levels of effort upto their knowledge frontier. In fact, given the sizeable relative contribution of teachers within the school education production function, reducing teachers' know-do gap is potentially the most direct mechanism through which principals can affect student outcomes. Empirical research has shown that, indeed, highly effective principals raise the achievement of a typical student in their schools by between two and seven months of learning in a single school year (Branch, Hanushek, and Rivkin 2013). Yet the pathways through which principals affect student outcomes have been underexplored thus far.

The study herein provides new evidence that suggests a strong association between the degree to which principals leverage their visibility position to monitor teachers and teachers' levels of substantive measures of effort, which in turn are predictive of student learning.

Roadmap to the Chapter

The next section turns to the Jordanian education sector. An overview of the education system in Jordan indicates the value of focusing on teacher effort to improve student outcomes in the country. The "Principal Monitoring and Teacher Effort" section uses evidence from a nationally representative sample of 156 schools in Jordan to test the association of principal monitoring and teacher effort. The "Monitoring, Teacher Effort, and Student Learning in Jordan" section specifically tests teacher effort as the pathway through which principal monitoring affects student learning. Lastly, the "Comparative Case Study in Jordanian Schools" section provides complementary evidence from a comparative case study to ease potential endogeneity concerns.

The Education Sector in Jordan

In the last two decades, Jordan has achieved close to universal primary enrollment (97 percent) and completion (93 percent), as well as high enrollment (88 percent) and completion (90 percent) rates at the secondary level that are on par with Organisation for Economic Co-Operation and Development (OECD) countries. Yet international student assessments keep refocusing the country's attention to what actually matters: student learning. In spite of high levels of educational attainment, 15-year-old Jordanians' average PISA mathematics, language, and science scores rank among the lowest of PISA-participating countries and economies (OECD 2012). Similarly, grade 8 students' average achievement in both mathematics and science nearly bottoms the list of Trends in International Mathematics and Science Study (TIMSS)-participating education systems (IEA 2011).

These indicators are somewhat unexpected given Jordan's internationally comparable expenditure levels in the education sector. Public education spending as a share of total government expenditure stood at roughly 10.3 percent in 2012 (World Bank 2016), slightly above the OECD average for that same year (9.8 percent), and on par with, for example, strong PISA-performers such as Germany, Austria, and Poland (figure 2.1). Furthermore, public education expenditure as a share of gross domestic product (GDP) was 3.4 percent in 2011 (World Bank 2016), just below the OECD average (5.2 percent), and yet at the same level as Singapore, Japan, and China's administrative regions of Macao SAR, China and Hong Kong SAR, China—the top-PISA-performers. Average PISA scores mask considerable within-country variability in student learning, however. For example, students at the top quartile in mathematics score as high as the OECD average, while those at the bottom quartile perform worse than their counterparts in all participating countries but Peru and Qatar (OECD 2012).

Figure 2.1 Public Education Expenditure as a Share of Total Government Expenditure and Average PISA Math Scores

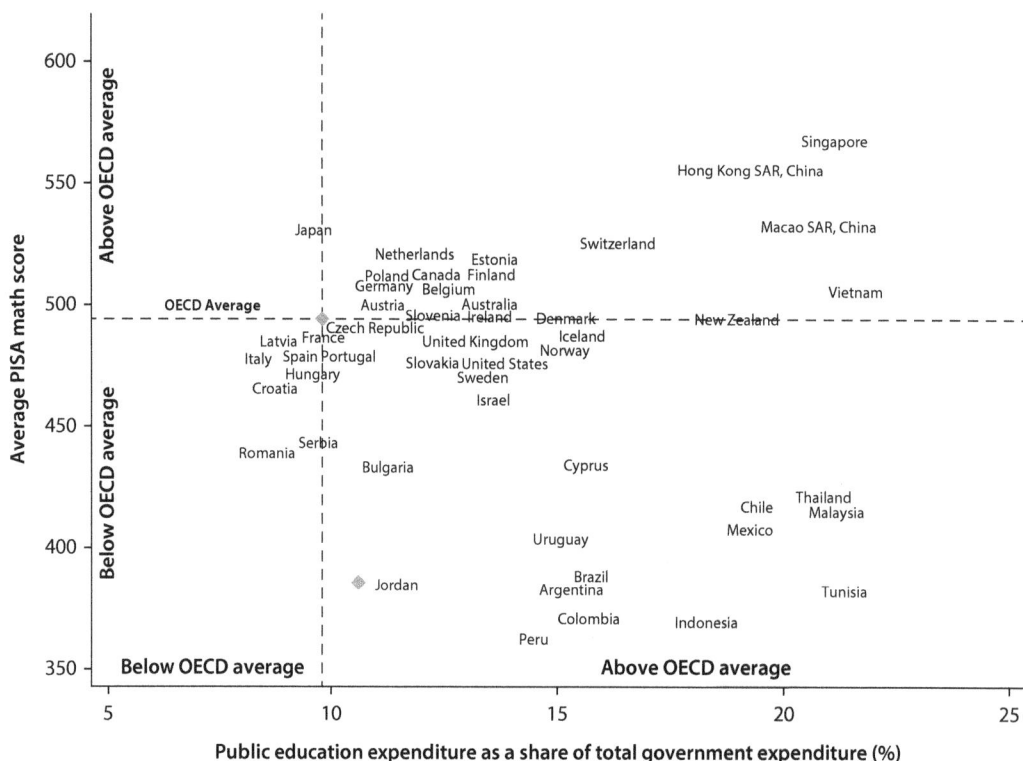

Sources: OECD 2012; World Bank 2012.
Note: 2011 expenditure data were used for Estonia, Canada, Poland, Belgium, Germany, Austria, Ireland, Slovenia, Denmark, Czech Republic, United Kingdom, Iceland, Norway, Portugal, Italy, Slovakia, United States, Sweden, Hungary, Croatia, Israel, Cyprus, Bulgaria, Malaysia, Mexico, and Uruguay.

The picture is not very different for language and science scores, suggesting size-able inequalities in student learning. These inequalities in student learning are unlikely to be attributed solely to differences in students' background and socio-economic status. In fact, the difference in Jordanian students' mathematics performance associated with a one-unit increase in the PISA index of economic, social, and cultural status (ESCS) is one of the smallest among PISA-participating countries and economies (OECD 2012).

This suggests that important drivers of the inequality in student learning might be found within schools. Yet an examination of the school production function suggests no sizeable insufficiencies in structural inputs.[1] School observations conducted in a nationally representative sample of schools in the country reveal basic school infrastructure to be almost universal, with 100 percent of schools having a source of electricity (97.4 percent functioning the day of the visit), all schools having working toilets or latrines (88.2 percent found to be very or somewhat clean), and roughly 90 percent of schools having a working drinking water source. Similarly, widespread availability of resources is found inside

Jordanian classrooms, with 96.7 percent equipped with a blackboard/whiteboard and 97.7 percent with chalk/markers. Classroom inventories also reveal 99.6 percent of students are provided with a desk or bench/chair arrangement, and almost all students have an Arabic language textbook (99.3 percent), a math textbook (97.7 percent), and a pen or pencil to write with (99.2 percent) (USAID 2012). With a cadre of over 80,000 teachers, the most important school input, average class size stands at 27,[2] on par with top PISA-performers such as the Republic of Korea and Japan, and just slightly above the OECD average of roughly 21 students per classroom (OECD 2012). Teacher educational attainment is adequate and without substantial variability, as the vast majority of teachers (83 percent) have a bachelor's degree or higher diploma, 12 percent have a diploma, and roughly 5 percent have a postgraduate degree (USAID 2012). Furthermore, available evidence on teacher training courses suggests a balance between pedagogical theory and methods with subject matter knowledge, whereby, for example, prospective primary school teachers spend 18 percent of their total training on pedagogy theory and methods, 27 percent of their time on mathematics, science, and language (9 percent each), and the remaining 55 percent of their time divided among six other subjects (social studies, English, computer science, art, physical education, Islamic learning) (World Bank 2010).

With adequate levels of structural school inputs and class size, and an arguably satisfactory teacher knowledge frontier, the value of focusing on teacher effort to improve and bridge the gap in student learning becomes essential. Are teachers in Jordan performing up to their knowledge frontier? Available evidence indicates that Jordan benefits from an average teacher absenteeism rate of only 2.6 percent,[3] on par with international standards. Moreover, classroom observations suggest that, on average, teachers spend barely 4.5 percent of classroom time on non-instructional activities, and that at virtually no time are teachers observed to be outside of the classroom during their lesson—again, on par with international standards (USAID 2012). Yet important differences in teacher quality may not be captured in these elementary measures of teacher effort. "Monitoring, Teacher Effort, and Student Learning in Jordan" section identifies four substantive measures of teacher effort in Jordan that are predictive of student learning, and for which there is significant variability across teachers in the country.

Principal Monitoring and Teacher Effort

Is Stronger Principal Monitoring Associated with Higher Teacher Effort?

The first hypothesis of this study is that higher levels of principal monitoring are associated with higher levels of teacher effort. To test this hypothesis, a multilevel model is estimated using data from a nationally representative sample of schools in Jordan. The results suggest that principal monitoring is indeed a strong predictor of teacher effort, but the estimates also suggest that the effect of principal monitoring is a function of principals' ability to observe teacher effort in a given effort area. The characteristics of the data, the empirical strategy used, and the results from the analysis are detailed below.

Data

The empirical analysis relies on data collected under the Student Performance in Reading and Mathematics, Pedagogic Practice, and School Management Study conducted by the United States Agency for International Development (USAID) in Jordan. Data were collected for a nationally representative sample comprising 156 schools, and field work was completed at the end of May 2012. Data sampling was carried out in three stages to minimize bias and ensure that the sample approximates wider population characteristics as closely as possible (see box 2.1 for sampling details).

For each school in the sample, the principal (or the assistant principal if the principal was not available) was automatically chosen to complete the School Principal Questionnaire as well as the School Observation Instrument. For each selected classroom, an external evaluator completed the Classroom Inventory Instrument and the classroom's teacher was automatically chosen to complete the Teacher Questionnaire. Last, each student in the sample completed the Student Questionnaire, the Early Grade Math Assessment (EGMA), and an Early Grade Reading Assessment (EGRA) Instruments. Table 2.1 summarizes the final count of the completed battery of instruments.

Empirical Strategy

To test the relationship between principal monitoring and teacher effort, a dataset is constructed by collapsing all school-, teacher-, and student-level variables in the USAID dataset at the teacher level. Next, a multilevel linear model that allows the intercept in the regression equation to vary by directorate and school is estimated. Such a model accounts for the hierarchical nature of the data, which is nested into four groupings—teachers, schools, directorates, and governorates.

Box 2.1 Sampling

In the first sampling stage, all primary schools listed in Jordan's Education Management Information System (EMIS) were stratified by region (North, Central, and South) and school-gender (all-boys, all-girls, and mixed schools), thus forming nine different strata. A random sample of schools was then selected proportional to the combined grade 2 and grade 3 enrollments as reported by the EMIS. This procedure resulted in a total of 156 randomly sampled schools.

During the second stage, classes/teachers were sampled within each selected school. In a given school, one grade 2 class was selected at random from all of the existing grade 2 classes (each with an equal probability of selection). The selection process was repeated for the third grade within each school, thus creating a sample of 156 randomly selected grade 2 classes and 156 randomly selected grade 3 classes.

The third sampling stage randomly selected 10 students within each class who were present on the day of the fieldwork. This process resulted in 1,529 randomly selected grade 2 students and 1,534 randomly selected grade 3 students.

Table 2.1 Study Instruments

Instrument	Level of administration	Total number of instruments completed
School Principal Questionnaire	School/principal	156
School Observation Instrument	School/principal	156
Teacher Questionnaire	Class/teacher	306
Classroom Inventory Instrument	Class/teacher	306
Student Questionnaire	Student	3,063
Early Grade Math Assessment	Student	3,063
Early Grade Reading Assessment	Student	3,063

Constructing a Principal Monitoring Index

A composite measure of a principal's level of teacher monitoring is constructed using: (1) a measure of the frequency by which a principal observes teachers in the classroom and (2) an indicator of the frequency by which she reviews teachers' lesson plans. Both measures are good indicators of the extent to which principals meet their key role of "following up with staff's daily performance," as stipulated by the Civil Service Bureau.[4]

Observing Teachers in the Classroom. Teachers were asked to recall how often their principals observed their teaching through a teacher survey. Answers were recorded in a seven-point measure as (0) never, (1) once a year, (2) once every 2–3 months, (3) once every month, (4) once every 2 weeks, (5) once every week, and (6) daily. Figure 2.2 shows the distribution of this measure in the sample. The majority of teachers (33.6 percent and 23.7 percent) reported that the principal conducted classroom observations once every 2–3 months, or once every month, respectively. Five percent reported never being observed by the principal when teaching, and only 0.7 percent reported being observed every single day.

Checking Teachers' Lesson Plans. Teachers were also asked to recall how often their principals checked their lesson plans. Answers were recorded in the same seven-point measure. The distribution for this variable is shown in figure 2.2. Most teachers (71.5 percent) reported that their lesson plans are checked by the principal once every week. Roughly 6 percent reported this to be a daily occurrence, while 2 percent of teachers recalled that this had never happened.

On their own, each of these measures provide information about two very specific types of monitoring mechanisms used by principals. However, the question at hand calls for an independent variable that provides a reasonable measure of the overall monitoring environment used by principals. As such, a composite measure—further referred to as *Principal Monitoring Index*—is constructed by adding together these two measures; it ranges from 0 to 12. If the *Principal Monitoring Index* variable takes on a value of 0, then a teacher reported that the principal never checks lesson plans or observes teaching. On the contrary, if the *Principal Monitoring Index* variable takes on a value of 12, then a teacher reported

Figure 2.2 Principal Monitoring Measures

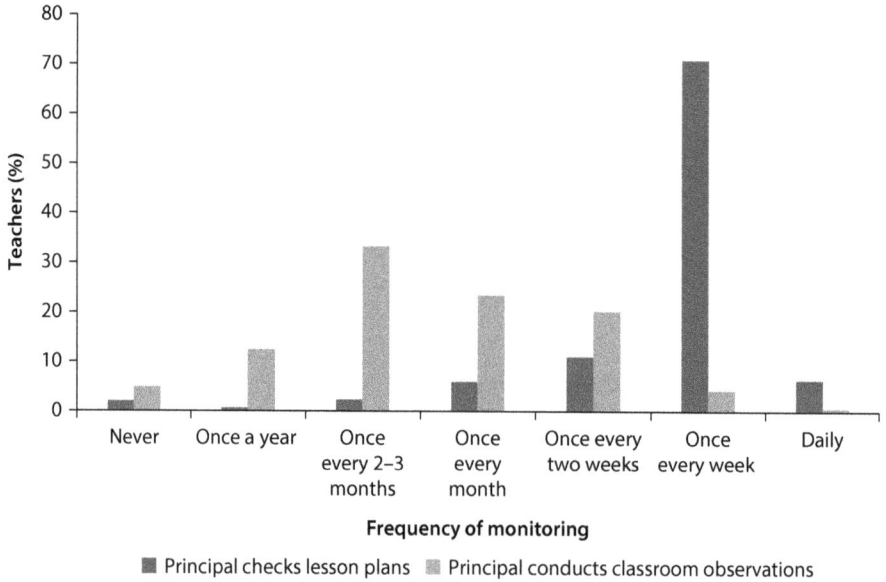

■ Principal checks lesson plans   ▦ Principal conducts classroom observations

Figure 2.3 Principal Monitoring Index

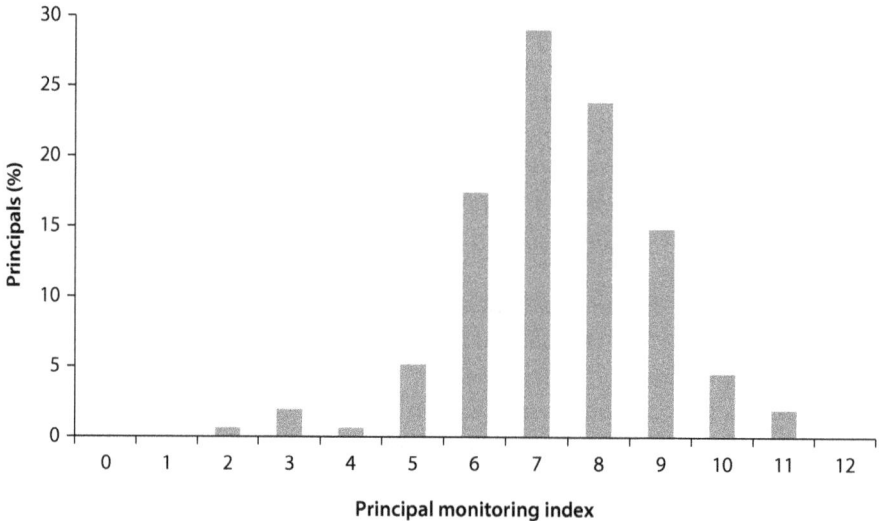

that the principal observes teaching and checks lesson plans every day. The composite measure provides a reasonable proxy for the overall monitoring environment since frequent teaching observation and lesson plan checking are likely to be correlated with frequent monitoring in other areas.[5] The distribution of this composite measure, shown in figure 2.3, reveals that almost 70 percent of schools have a *Principal Monitoring Index* that ranges somewhere between 6 and 8,

Box 2.2 Limitations of the Principal Monitoring Index

An important shortcoming of this index is that it only captures the monitoring function of principal accountability. Arguably, principal accountability requires that principals both monitor teacher performance and, as a function of the information they gather through monitoring, reward or penalize teachers to incentivize higher effort. The dataset, however, provides no good proxy for incentives, thus leading this study to limit its independent variable of interest to principal monitoring. The "Comparative Case Study in Jordanian Schools" section addresses this limitation, presenting results from a qualitative study aimed at disentangling the effect that each of the two accountability functions—monitoring and enforcement— could potentially have on teacher effort.

while 9 percent of schools score below 6 in the index, and 21 percent have an outstanding monitoring index that is above 8 (see box 2.2 for some limitations of this index).

Measuring Teacher Effort

In guiding the selection of the dependent variables for the study, a set of four measures of teacher effort matching each of three domains of the FFT were identified from the USAID dataset. This dataset, which is aligned with teacher professional standards in Jordan, as stipulated by the Civil Service Bureau, in turn corresponds with each of the three domains of the FFT[6]—an internationally used and comprehensive framework developed by education expert Charlotte Danielson to assess teachers' practices.

The first variable—*Creating an Environment of Respect and Rapport*—matches the national teacher standard on treating students with courtesy and falls under FFT's Classroom Environment Domain. The second variable—*Providing Feedback to Students*—matches the teacher standard on grading students' assignments and falls under FFT's Instruction Domain. The third variable—*Designing Student Assessment*—matches Jordan's teacher standard on using effective educational strategies and evaluation methods and falls under FFT's Planning and Preparation Domain. The fourth variable—*Designing Coherent Instruction*—matches the teacher standard on planning for effective learning considering students' individual differences and falls under FFT's Planning and Preparation Domain. As shown in figure 2.4, a reasonable degree of heterogeneity in observability exists in the selected variables, with those pertaining to the Planning and Preparation Domain mostly requiring the exertion of teacher effort outside of the classroom, and those relating to the Classroom Environment and the Instruction Domains necessitating teachers' daily effort inside the classroom. If principal monitoring is indeed a strong predictor of teacher effort, it should be expected that such association be a function of the degree of observability in the different measures of effort.

Figure 2.4 Measures of Teacher Effort Mapped against the FFT

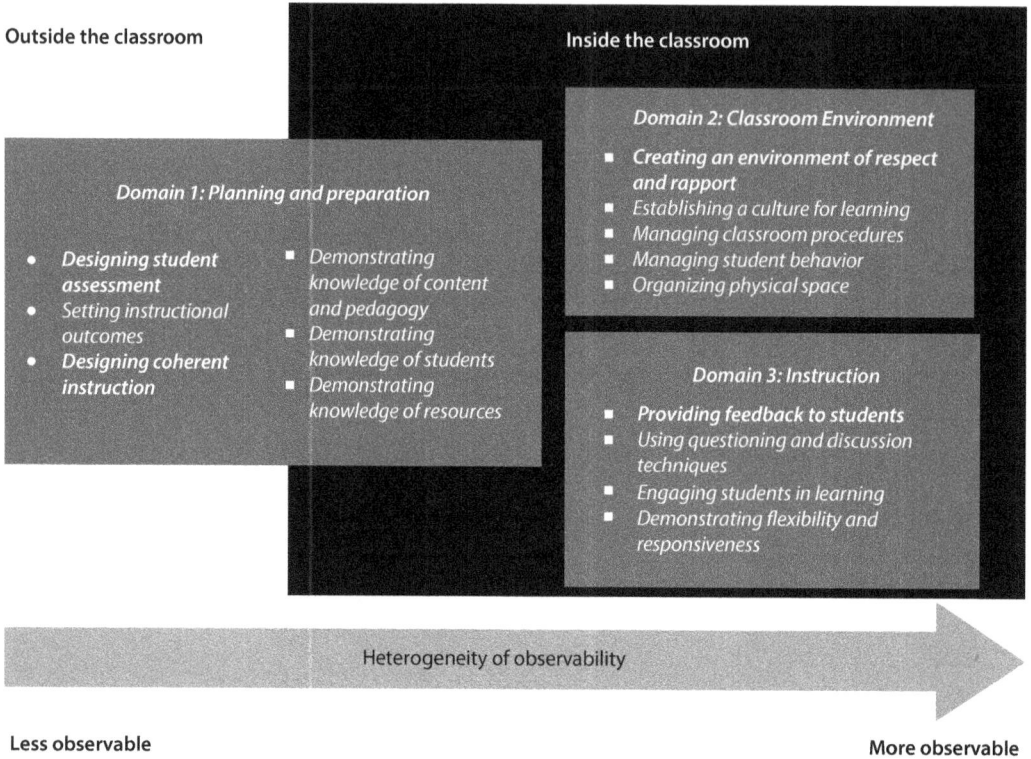

Outside the classroom

Inside the classroom

Domain 2: Classroom Environment

- *Creating an environment of respect and rapport*
- *Establishing a culture for learning*
- *Managing classroom procedures*
- *Managing student behavior*
- *Organizing physical space*

Domain 1: Planning and preparation

- *Designing student assessment*
- *Setting instructional outcomes*
- *Designing coherent instruction*

- *Demonstrating knowledge of content and pedagogy*
- *Demonstrating knowledge of students*
- *Demonstrating knowledge of resources*

Domain 3: Instruction

- *Providing feedback to students*
- *Using questioning and discussion techniques*
- *Engaging students in learning*
- *Demonstrating flexibility and responsiveness*

Heterogeneity of observability

Less observable   More observable

The four selected measures of teacher effort are described in table 2.2 (box 2.3 presents caveats to these measures, and box 2.4 shows bivariate correlations among the different measures of teacher effort).

Variability in Teacher Effort

It was previously noted that given their small variability, elementary measures of teacher effort such as teacher absenteeism and classroom time allocation were unable to capture any meaningful differences in teacher quality in Jordan. Contrariwise, an important degree of variability exists in the four more substantive measures of effort among teachers in the sample.

Creating an Environment of Respect and Rapport. Interviews with students revealed important differences in the extent to which teachers strive to create an environment of respect and rapport in their classrooms. As shown in figure 2.5, when a student is unable to answer a question, almost a fourth of teachers try to create a positive environment by explaining or rephrasing the question, encouraging the student to try again, or correcting the student without scolding her. However, as many as 70 percent of teachers are reported to simply repeat the exact same question to the same student again, or to ask another student instead,

Table 2.2 Measures of Teacher Effort

Measure of teacher effort	Description and scale	Source
Creating an environment of respect and rapport	This variable is proxied through an ordinal measure of how a teacher responds when a student is unable to answer a question during instruction. Higher values represent higher levels of teacher effort in responding to students in a way that is more conducive to creating a respectful and emotionally supportive environment for learning, while lower values represent the opposite. Specifically, this variable ranges from 0 to 2. A score of 2 is assigned in cases where the student reports that the teacher rephrases/explains the question, encourages the student to try again, or corrects the student but does not scold him/her. A score of 1 is assigned in cases where the student reports that the teacher asks another student or the teacher asks the same student the exact same question. A score of 0 is assigned in cases where the student reports that the teacher scolds the student, sends the student outside of the classroom, hits the student, or sends the student to the corner of the classroom.	Data for this variable were collected based on interviews with 10 randomly selected students in each sampled classroom.
Providing feedback to students	This variable is proxied through an ordinal measure that measures how many comments or corrections a teacher provides in each student's Arabic language copybook. The variable ranges from 0 to 4, with higher values representing higher teacher effort in providing comments or corrections more frequently, and lower values representing fewer to no marks in students' copybooks.	Data for this variable were collected by an external observer who visited classrooms and examined the Arabic language copybook of 10 randomly selected students per classroom.
Designing student assessments	This variable is proxied through an ordinal measure denoting how many of the following assessment methods a teacher uses to monitor student learning and to provide a variety of performance opportunities for students: written tests, oral evaluations, homework, worksheets, end-of-semester evaluations, projects/portfolios, and debates. The variable ranges from 0 to 7.	Data for this variable were collected based on surveys administered to every teacher in each sampled classroom.
Designing coherent instruction	This variable is proxied through a dichotomous measure denoting whether a teacher uses student assessments to inform the design of her lesson plan. Teachers who consider specific student performance and needs while designing lessons are considered to put forth more effort since creating tailored lesson plans takes more forethought and effort than just using a "one-size fits all" lesson plan.	Data for this variable were collected based on surveys administered to every teacher in each sampled classroom.

Box 2.3 Caveat for Teacher Effort Measures

It is to be noted that the Designing Student Assessment and Designing Coherent Instruction variables are measured through teacher surveys. As such, they are likely to be subject to social desirability bias—a tendency of survey respondents (that is, teachers) to answer questions in a manner that will be viewed favorably by others. Yet the sizeable proportion of teachers in the sample who provided answers for these two measures that are viewed negatively for the purposes of this study may suggest only a modest interference of this bias with the interpretation of the study results.

Box 2.4 Bivariate Correlations among Measures of Teacher Effort

Having identified these four different measures of teacher effort, it is important to consider the bivariate correlations between them. If the correlation between the dependent variables is low, then it is likely that the four different measures are accounting for distinct aspects of teacher effort. Having uncorrelated measures of teacher effort is important since it will allow the analysis to determine how principal monitoring is associated with teacher effort on a variety of dimensions. The correlations between the different measures of teacher effort are provided in table 2.3. The strongest correlation (at 0.347) exists between the Designing Student Assessment variable and the Designing Coherent Instruction variable. The moderate correlation between these two variables is not surprising, since both of these measures proxy how much effort a teacher puts into planning and preparing for her lesson by designing student assessments that can help her inform her instruction. Aside from this, most of the other correlations are weak. This set of results suggests that the different dependent variables are indeed measuring distinct aspects of teacher effort.

Figure 2.5 Creating an Environment of Respect and Rapport

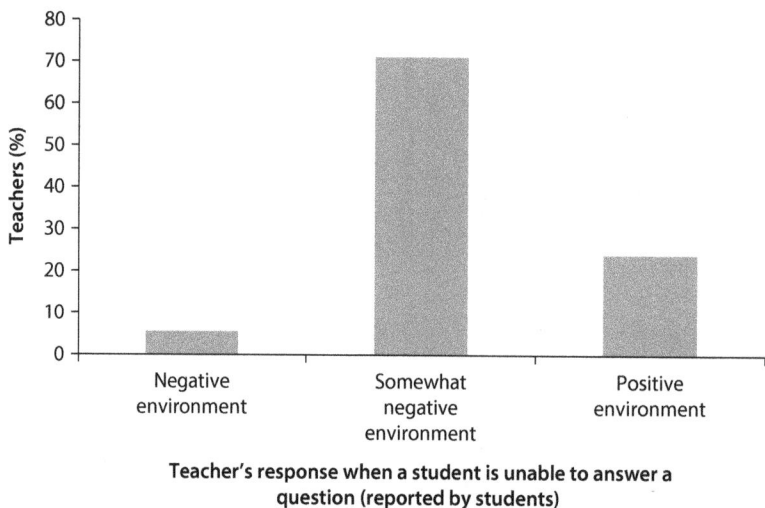

Teacher's response when a student is unable to answer a
question (reported by students)

Table 2.3 Correlation between Measures of Teacher Effort

	Providing feedback to students	Environment of respect and rapport	Designing student assessment	Designing coherent instruction
Providing feedback to students	1.000***			
Environment of respect and rapport	0.046**	1.000***		
Designing student assessment	0.080**	0.219***	1.000***	
Designing coherent instruction	0.107***	−0.048**	0.347***	1.000***

*p < .10; **p < .05; ***p < .01.

while 5.4 percent of teachers are reported to scold students, hit them, or send them outside of the classroom or to stand in a corner if they fail to give the right answer to a question.

Providing Feedback to Students. Variability is also observed in the effort put forth by teachers in providing feedback to their students, as shown in figure 2.6. Roughly one-fifth of all teachers had marked all pages of their students' copybooks, and almost half of them had marked most pages. One-fourth of all teachers, however, had marked only a few pages of the copybook and 3.4 percent of them had not marked even a single page.

Designing Student Assessments. Interview answers also recorded varying levels of effort exerted by teachers in designing assessment methods for their students. Almost two-thirds of teachers report using only one or two methods of student assessment, while around 20 percent report using three methods, and roughly 15 percent of teachers report using more than four methods to assess their students. Only 1.6 percent of teachers report not using any method of student assessment whatsoever (figure 2.7).

Designing Coherent Instruction. As seen in figure 2.8, only one-fourth of teachers report using student assessments to inform their lesson planning, with the great majority (75.7 percent) reporting to be agnostic to it.

Heterogeneity in the Observability of Teacher Effort

Discerning where each of the above four measures of teacher effort falls on the observability spectrum merits special consideration. At one extreme of the observability spectrum, *Creating an Environment of Respect and Rapport* is mainly determined by teachers' effort in interacting in a positive and supportive tone with their students, which can be observed within the classroom on a daily basis. As such, a strong and positive relationship is to be expected between principal monitoring and teacher effort in *Creating an Environment of Respect and Rapport*. Similarly, a strong and positive association is expected between principal monitoring and teacher effort in providing feedback to students, as this requires teachers to have a "finger on the pulse" of a lesson, and to monitor student learning

The Last Mile to Quality Service Delivery in Jordan • http://dx.doi.org/10.1596/978-1-4648-1069-5

Figure 2.6 Providing Feedback to Students

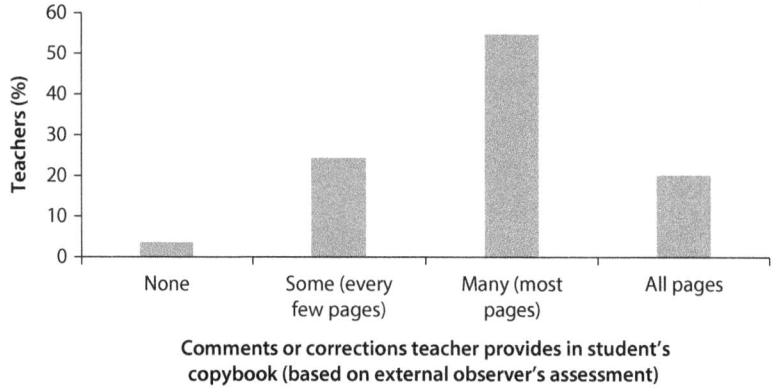

Comments or corrections teacher provides in student's
copybook (based on external observer's assessment)

Figure 2.7 Designing Student Assessments

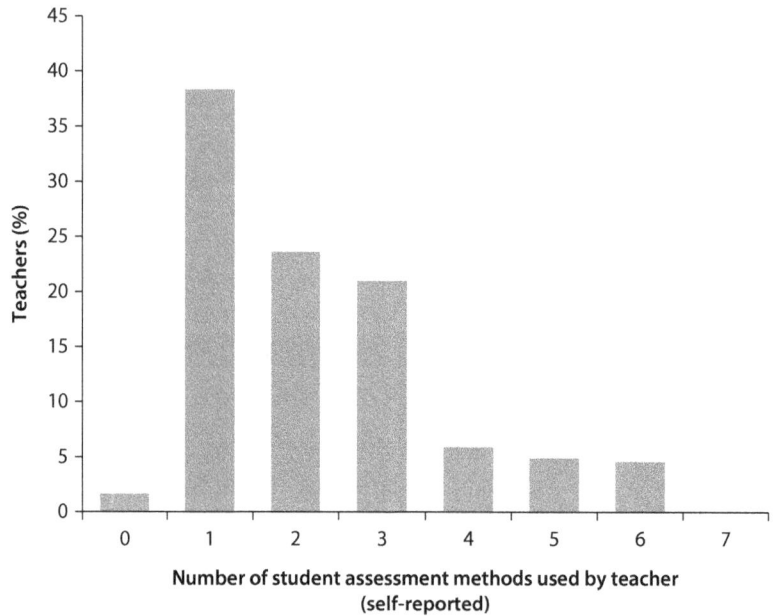

Number of student assessment methods used by teacher
(self-reported)

on a daily basis. This daily imperative allows principals to conduct random class-room visits on any day and expect to see students' copybooks to be marked.

Somewhere in the middle of the spectrum, teacher effort in designing student assessment can be more challenging for principals to observe. Teacher effort in this area is mostly exerted outside of the classroom at determined intervals throughout the academic term. For example, the use of a rich set of

Figure 2.8 Designing Coherent Instruction

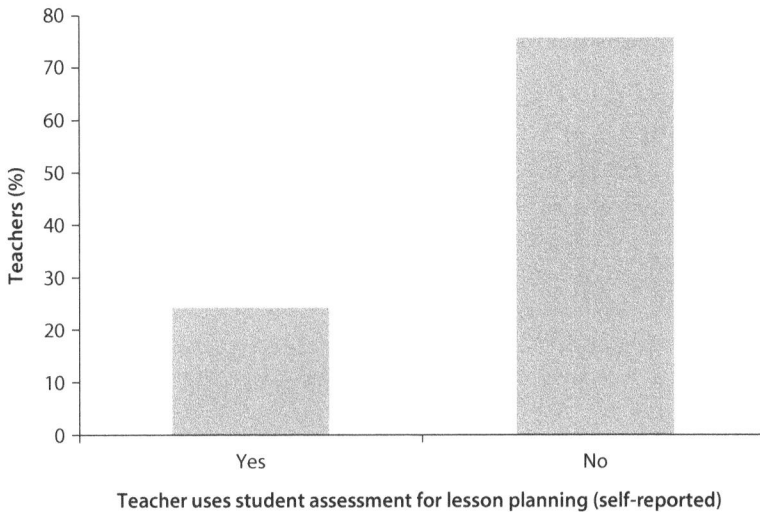

Teacher uses student assessment for lesson planning (self-reported)

assessments that provide a variety of performance opportunities for students requires effort at the design stage of such assessments, before the start of the academic term, and/or before determined assessment intervals during the term. Furthermore, it requires periodic effort in implementing the designed assessments, such as administering oral and written exams and assessing student debates, presentations, and projects. As it takes place mostly outside of the classroom, and is implemented intermittently throughout the academic term, teacher effort in this realm is difficult to observe in its full breadth through a limited number of classroom observations. As such, a positive but weaker relationship is to be expected between principal monitoring and teacher effort in designing student assessment.

Last, at the other extreme of the observability spectrum, teacher effort in designing coherent instruction is likely to be one of the hardest areas for principals to observe. If designing—and implementing—student assessments is already difficult to observe, determining the extent to which the information gathered through these assessments is used by teachers to inform the design of a coherent lesson plan that responds to students' learning needs can be even more formidable. Effort that teachers put in planning for their lessons happen almost exclusively outside of the classroom, and although principals can observe their teaching during a class or request to read their lesson planning records, determining just how much effort a teacher puts into designing a lesson plan that is actually relevant to her student needs seems extremely difficult. Thus the constructed principal monitoring index should have only a very weak relationship with teacher effort in this realm.

Control Variables

A variety of factors are likely to confound the relationship between principal monitoring and teacher effort. These factors are related to teachers' knowledge frontier, the socioeconomic status of each school and its students, other monitoring mechanisms used by actors other than the school principal, and specific school characteristics. As described in table 2.4, measures for all of these factors have been included in the analysis to account for potential confounding effects. Descriptive statistics for all of the variables used in the analysis are presented in table A.2.

Results

Results from the analysis are presented in table A.3, which provides estimates from four sets of models. Models 1–3 estimate the relationship between principal monitoring and teacher effort in *Providing Feedback to Students*. Models 4–6 test

Table 2.4 Control Variables

Set of control variables	Description of specific variables	Explanation of potential confounding effects
Teachers' knowledge frontier	The analysis includes: (1) an ordinal measure of a teacher's highest level of education, (2) a dichotomous variable that denotes if a teacher received pre-service training in how to teach reading, and (3) an indicator variable that denotes if a teacher received pre-service training in how to teach math. The analysis is unable to control for a teacher's years of experience, as this information was not collected in the fieldwork.	Controlling for a teacher's level of knowledge is important since highly qualified teachers may self-select themselves into schools with highly competent and motivated principals.
Socioeconomic status of schools and students	The analysis includes: (1) a variable that denotes if a school receives government aid, (2) a variable measuring whether a student's family owns a computer, and (3) a variable that represents how wealthy a school is relative to other schools in Jordan.	Controlling for differences in socioeconomic status across students and schools is important since principals and teachers who exert higher levels of effort could self-select themselves into better resourced schools and/or schools in higher-income neighborhoods.
Other types of monitoring mechanisms	The analysis controls for "top-down" monitoring by including: (1) an ordinal variable that records how many times a school has been visited by a directorate inspector as reported by the principal, and (2) an ordinal variable that measures how often a teacher has been observed teaching by a directorate supervisor as reported by the teacher. It also controls for monitoring coming from the community and/or parents ("bottom-up") by including (3) an ordinal variable that captures how frequently the parent teacher association met during the past school year, as reported by the principal.	It is essential to account for other types of monitoring because principals are likely to increase their monitoring activities when they perceive that other actors are highly concerned with teacher effort.
Other school/class characteristics	The analysis includes: (1) a dichotomous variable denoting if a school is located in a rural district, (2) an ordinal variable that records the gender of a school (that is, all boys, all girls, or mixed), and (3) a variable that records the teacher-student ratio in each class.	It is standard to control for specific school/class characteristics.

this relationship with *Creating an Environment of Respect and Rapport* as the dependent variable. The relationships between principal monitoring and the design of student assessment and the design of coherent instruction are estimated in Models 7–9 and 10–12, respectively. Each set of estimates provides results from a number of models to test whether the results are robust to model specification. Findings from these models are discussed below.

Teachers Who Are Frequently Monitored Are More Likely to Provide Feedback to Their Students

In Models 1–3, the coefficient for the *Principal Monitoring Index* variable is positive and statistically significant at the 95 percent confidence level, suggesting that teachers are more likely to provide frequent comments/corrections in their students' Arabic language copybook when there is a high level of monitoring by the principal. Substantively, as shown in table 2.5, a 1.0 SD increase in the *Principal Monitoring Index* variable corresponds to a 0.14 SD increase in teacher effort in providing feedback to students.

More Effort in Creating a Positive Learning Environment Is Put Forth by Teachers Who Are Monitored More Often

The results in Models 4–6 suggest that a strong and positive relationship exists between principal monitoring and teacher effort in creating a climate of respect and rapport. The coefficient for the Principal Monitoring Index variable is positive and statistically significant in all three models, such that a 1.0 SD increase in this index corresponds to a 0.09 SD increase in teacher effort in creating a positive learning environment for students.

As Anticipated, Higher Principal Monitoring Is Weakly Predictive of Teacher Effort in Designing Student Assessment and Not Predictive of Designing Coherent Instruction

In Models 7–9, the coefficient for the Principal Monitoring Index variable is positive but just misses statistical significance with p-values of 0.111, 0.134, and 0.110, respectively. This set of results suggests that teachers may be more likely to put forth effort in designing and using a variety of student assessment methods when they are monitored frequently by their principal. In Models 10–12, the coefficient for the Principal Monitoring Index variable is positive but statistically significant in just one model, suggesting no robust empirical relationship between

Table 2.5 Substantive Effects—Principal Monitoring and Teacher Effort

Providing feedback to students	Environment of respect and rapport	Designing student assessment	Designing coherent instruction
0.145	0.090	0.048	0.082
[0.046, 0.242]	[0.000, 0.178]	[−0.003, 0.099]	[0.003, 0.159]
(0.033, 0.261)	(−0.022, 0.194)	(−0.010, 0.108)	(−0.007, 0.174)

Note: The 90 percent confidence intervals are in brackets. The 95 percent confidence intervals are in parentheses. Estimates were produced from Models 3, 6, 9, and 12 in table A.3.

principal monitoring and the likelihood that a teacher will put forth effort to use student assessments to inform the design of her instruction.

Overall, Principal Monitoring Is Strongly Associated with Teacher Effort, Yet Such Association Is a Function of the Extent to Which Different Measures of Teacher Effort Are Observable to Principals

The empirical analysis suggests that higher levels of monitoring by principals have a strong and positive association with teachers' effort in *Providing Feedback to Students* and *Creating an Environment of Respect and Rapport*—both measures of teacher effort that fall on the right side of the observability spectrum. Furthermore, the results suggest that a weaker, but still positive, relationship exists between principal monitoring and teacher effort in designing student assessments. The inability of the Principal Monitoring Index variable to achieve statistical significance in Models 7–9 is not surprising, since observing just how rich a teacher's assessment methods are is somewhat difficult for a principal to do with a limited number of classroom observations.

The analysis suggests that no robust relationship exists between principal monitoring and teacher effort in designing coherent instruction. This empirical result is also not surprising as it is extremely difficult for principals to observe just how much effort a teacher puts into lesson plans. With this last measure of teacher effort falling on the left side of the observability spectrum, there is no reason to expect that frequent monitoring by principals will increase teacher effort in the context of lesson planning.

Monitoring, Teacher Effort, and Student Learning in Jordan

Is Stronger Principal Monitoring Also Associated with Higher Student Learning?

The results presented thus far suggest that teachers are more likely to exert higher levels of effort (in areas where effort is actually observable) when they are monitored frequently by their principals. Yet the critical question is whether principal monitoring is actually associated with better student learning. Empirical research has shown that highly effective principals raise the achievement of a typical student in their schools by between two and seven months of learning in a single school year (Branch, Hanushek, and Rivkin 2013). But the pathways through which principals affect student outcomes have been underexplored thus far. This study posits that reducing teachers' know-do gap through higher levels of monitoring could potentially be the most direct mechanism through which principals can affect student outcomes. Specifically, the second hypothesis of this study is that principal monitoring is associated with better student learning and that this association is mediated by teacher effort. To test this hypothesis, a multilevel mediation analysis is conducted. The results suggest that principal monitoring is indeed strongly associated with student learning and that such association is mediated by those areas of teacher effort that are observable to the principal.

Empirical Strategy

To test the relationship between principal monitoring and student learning, and its potential mediation by teacher effort, a dataset is constructed by disaggregating all variables from the previous analysis at the student level. Next, a multilevel mediation analysis is conducted to account for the hierarchical nature of the data. Principal monitoring can affect student learning through two potential pathways. First, it is possible that principal monitoring may have a positive impact on student academic performance because of its influence on increased teacher effort. In addition to this indirect effect, it is possible that principal monitoring can directly influence student learning (figure 2.9 illustrates these two pathways). The conducted mediation analysis considers the possibility that principal monitoring has both a direct and an indirect association with student learning. (See box 2.5 for a methodological note on the mediation analysis).

Figure 2.9 Causal Pathways of Principal Monitoring on Student Learning

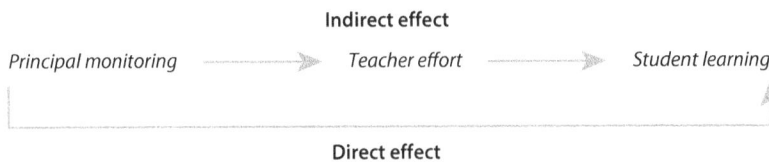

Indirect effect

Principal monitoring → Teacher effort → Student learning

Direct effect

Box 2.5 Multilevel Mediation Analysis

To conduct the multilevel mediation analysis, Hicks and Tingley's (2011) mediation package in R is used to calculate the average mediation and direct effects by simulating predicted values of the mediator or outcome variable, which are not observable, and then calculating the appropriate quantities of interest (average causal mediation, direct effects, and total effects). This allows for the implementation of Imai, Keele, and Tingley's (2010) four-step parametric algorithm: (1) fitting models for the observed outcome and mediator variables; (2) simulating model parameters from their sampling distribution; (3) simulating potential values of the mediator, calculating potential outcomes given simulated values of the mediator, and computing quantities of interest for each draw of model parameters; and (4) computing summary statistics (Hicks and Tingley 2011).

The hierarchical nature of the data poses a challenge for mediation analysis. Computational limitations only allow for mediation analysis to be conducted including one random effect into the model (for either the teacher, school, or directorate level). Because the intra-class correlation is likely to be highest at the school level (Duflo, Hanna, and Ryan 2012; Imberman 2011; Lavy, Paserman, and Schlasser 2011), the mediation analysis is conducted while accounting for clustering at this level. As a robustness check, results from an analysis that accounts for clustering at the class level are also presented.

box continues next page

Box 2.5 Multilevel Mediation Analysis *(continued)*

A final note to be made is about the sequential ignorability (SI) assumption—a necessary assumption to achieve identification in mediation analysis. The SI assumption comprises two assumptions: first, the independent variable is assumed to be statistically independent of potential outcomes and potential mediating variables; and second, the mediating variable is assumed to be exogenous conditional on pretreatment confounders and the independent variable of interest (Hicks and Tingley 2011). As these two assumptions are rarely satisfied in applied research, it is important to determine how sensitive estimates are to violations of SI. A discussion of how robust the mediation analysis results presented below are to violations of SI is provided in box 2.6 and appendix B.

Independent Variable: Principal Monitoring

As with the analysis in the "Monitoring, Teacher Effort, and Student Learning in Jordan" section, the independent variable of interest for the mediation analysis is the Principal Monitoring Index—a composite measure of a principal's level of teacher monitoring. Using the Principal Monitoring Index variable, the analysis is able to determine specifically how principal monitoring is associated with student outcomes.

Measuring Student Outcomes. Principals' role in teacher accountability systems is as important as its contribution to ensuring that student outcomes are a product of increasing levels of teacher effort in desirable teaching practices that are conducive to actual student learning, and not of perverse teacher practices that simply promote rote memorization.

As such, two pairs of measures of student outcomes are used as dependent variables for this analysis. The first pair are test scores measuring language skills, while the latter pair are test scores that assess mathematics skills. Each pair includes one score that measures basic automaticity and, thus, is likely to be subject to rote memorization. This is paired with a second score that measures conceptual understanding and application of key concepts to new situations, and that is likely to represent actual student learning.

Students' Language Skills. To measure students' language skills, the analysis uses two main variables. First, a variable that denotes the percent of letter sounds a student correctly identifies (letter sound knowledge) is used to measure student outcomes in basic language automaticity that are likely to be subject to rote memorization. As seen in figure 2.10, significant variance exists in student outcomes for this variable, with an average of 33.4 percent of questions correctly answered and an SD of 21.3. At one end of the distribution, roughly 15 percent of students correctly answered more than half of the questions, while at the other end of the distribution, one-third of students provided correct answers to only 10 percent of the questions.

Second, the reading comprehension variable is used to measure student outcomes in language skills that require a conceptual understanding and are likely

Figure 2.10 Letter Sound Knowledge

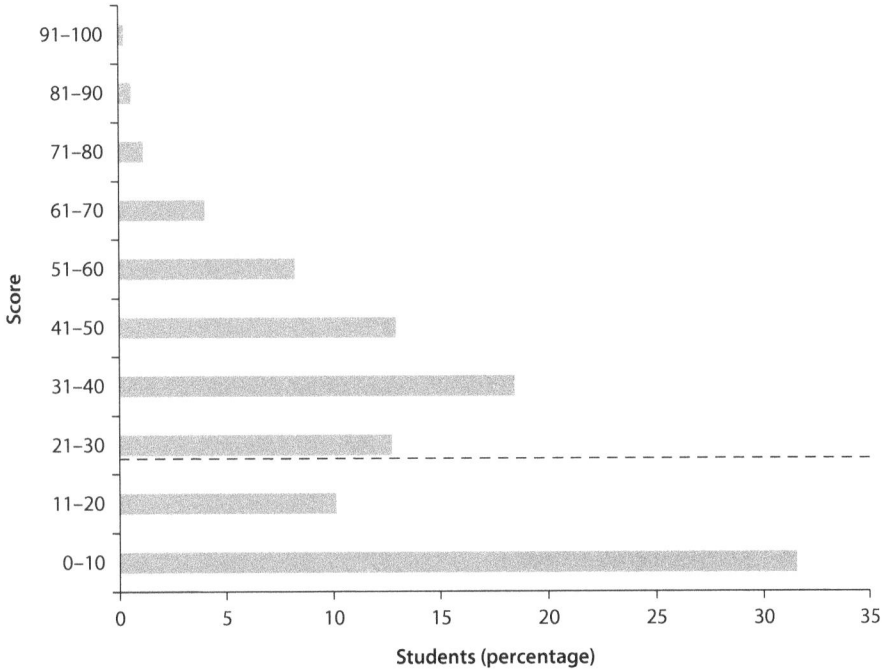

to represent actual student learning. Students were given a passage to read, and then asked to answer questions related to the passage. Half of the students in the sample were able to correctly answer as little as 20 percent of the questions they were asked, below the average of 26.1 percent, meaning the distribution was fairly skewed. In contrast, 7.5 percent of students correctly responded to all of the questions, and almost 20 percent of them provided accurate answers for 60–80 percent of the questions (figure 2.11).

Students' Mathematic Skills. Two other variables are used to measure students' skills in mathematics. First, a variable that denotes the percent of a selection of one- to three-digit numbers a student correctly identifies (number identification) is used to measure student outcomes in basic number automaticity that are likely to be subject to rote memorization. Relative to the other variables, little variance exists in the data for this variable. As illustrated in figure 2.12, half of the students in the sample accurately identified 80 percent or more of the digits they were presented with, and as few as a fifth of them correctly identified less than 50 percent of the digits.

Second, the word problems variable is used to measure students' conceptual understanding of key mathematical concepts by presenting them three situations in words, and asking them to make a plan and solve the problems through any mathematical solution they can think of. Contrary to the number identification variable, the word problems variable presents significant variance in the data,

Figure 2.11 Reading Comprehension

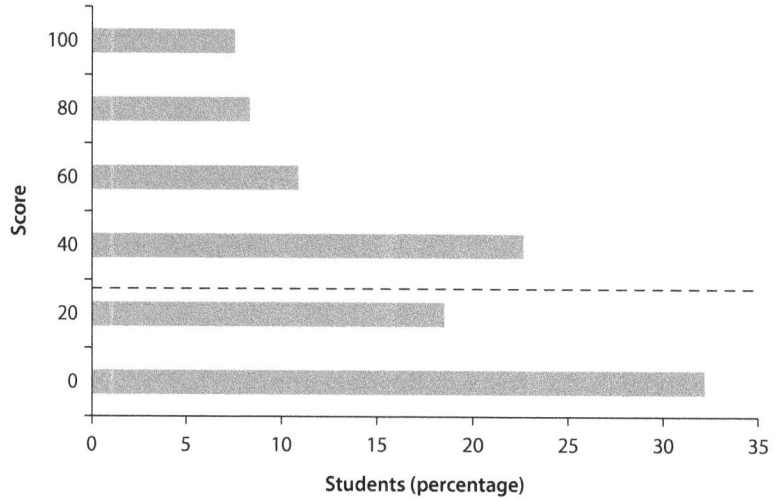

Figure 2.12 Number Identification

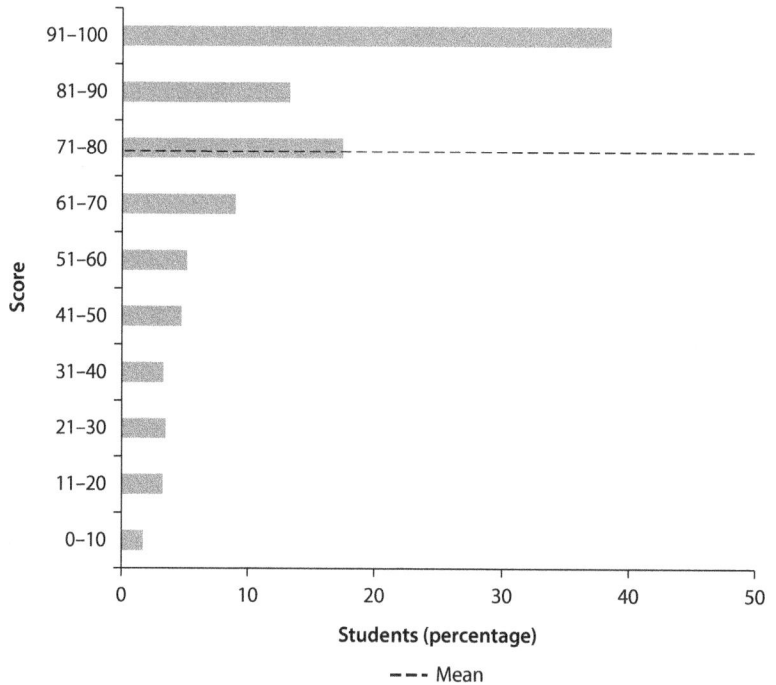

--- Mean

with almost a third of students unable to correctly answer even a single question, roughly 50 percent of students correctly answering one or two of the questions, and only 14 percent correctly responding to all three word problem questions (figure 2.13).

The four selected measures of student outcomes are described in table 2.6.

Figure 2.13 Word Problems

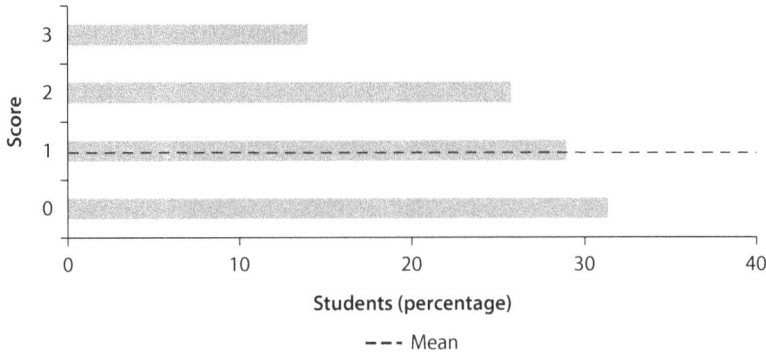

Table 2.6 Measures of Student Outcomes

Measure of student outcomes	Description and scale	Source
Language skills		
Letter sound knowledge[a]	Students were shown a chart containing 10 rows each with 10 letters arranged randomly, yielding a total of 100 letters. Students were then asked to produce the sounds associated with each letter as quickly and accurately as they could within one minute, yielding a score of correct letters per minute. As such, the variable denotes the percent of letter sounds a student correctly identified.	Data from this variable were collected based on the Early Grade Reading Assessment (EGRA) administered by United States Agency for International Development (USAID) examiners to the 10 randomly selected students in each sampled classroom.
Reading comprehension[b]	Students were given a passage to read, and after a minute, the passage was removed. Students were then orally asked questions that required them to answer basic facts or inferential questions based on the passage they read. The variable is the number of correct answers by the student, with a maximum possible score of 6.	Data from this variable were collected based on the EGRA administered by USAID examiners to the 10 randomly selected students in each sampled classroom.
Math skills		
Number identification[a]	Students were given 30 seconds to orally identify one- to three-digit numbers arranged in order of increasing difficulty presented in a grid. Thus, the variable measures the percent of number identification questions answered correctly.	Data from this variable were collected based on the Early Grade Mathematics Assessment (EGMA) administered by USAID examiners to the 10 randomly selected students in each sampled classroom.
Word problems[b]	Students were presented with three situations in words, and asked to make a plan and solve the problems through any mathematical solution they could think of. The variable provides a three-point measure of a student's ability to correctly answer word problems in mathematics.	Data from this variable were collected based on the EGMA administered by USAID examiners to the 10 randomly selected students in each sampled classroom.

a. Measures of basic automaticity, likely to be subject to rote memorization.
b. Measures of conceptual understanding and application of key concepts to new situations, likely to represent actual student learning.

Mediating Variable: Teacher Effort

The mediating variables are the four measures of teacher effort used in the analysis in the "Monitoring, Teacher Effort, and Student Learning in Jordan" section: creating an environment of respect and rapport, providing feedback to students, designing student assessments, and designing coherent instruction. Multiple teacher effort measures are again used to ensure that teacher effort is measured across a variety of areas. To ensure that the results are robust for the mediation analysis, a large number of tests are conducted by considering every unique combination of student outcomes and teacher effort variables.

The heterogeneity in the observability of teacher effort has important implications for the mediation analysis. Since principal monitoring is very weakly associated with teacher effort in areas where effort is difficult to observe, it is expected that monitoring will also have less of an indirect association on student learning when considered through such mediators (that is, the designing student assessments, and designing coherent instruction variables).

In contrast, if principal monitoring has a strong and positive association on teacher effort in a given area, then higher levels of principal monitoring are expected to be associated with student outcomes through these mediators (that is, the creating an environment of respect and rapport, providing feedback to students variables).

Control Variables

A variety of factors are likely to confound the relationship between principal monitoring and student outcomes. These factors are related to students' and schools' socioeconomic status, and to the extent to which students receive academic support outside of school. As described in table 2.7, measures for these factors were

Table 2.7 Control Variables Included in the Mediation Analysis

Set of control variables	Description of specific variables	Explanation of potential confounding effects
Socioeconomic status of students and schools	Four variables were included into the analysis to control for a student's socioeconomic status: (1) a variable that denotes if a student has a radio in his household, (2) a variable that denotes if a student's family owns a car, (3) a variable that denotes if a student has a computer in his household, and (4) a variable that denotes if a student receives free meals at school.	Controlling for differences in socioeconomic status across students and schools is important since high-performing principals, teachers, and students could self-select themselves into better resourced schools.
Academic support outside of school	Two variables were included in the analysis: (1) a variable is used to denote whether a student receives help with her homework at home, and (2) another variable is used to denote if a student receives private lessons after school.	Closely related to the first set of control variables, this set of variables stems from the strong and well-documented association between family background and student achievement (Bornstein and Bradley 2003; Brooks-Gunn and Duncan 1997; Coleman 1988; Sirin 2005). Namely, parents with higher socioeconomic status are more likely to provide their children with a stimulating home environment to promote cognitive development and better school outcomes.

Box 2.6 Robustness Check and Sensitivity Analysis

The mediation analysis presented in table A.5 accounts for clustering at the school level. Table A.6 presents results from an additional mediation analysis that accounts for clustering at the class level. The latter suggests that the empirical conclusions herewith are relatively robust to changes in the way in which clustering is accounted for.

From another perspective, and as noted in box 2.5, the SI assumption is necessary to achieve identification in mediation analysis. Since SI is likely to be violated in the data, a sensitivity analysis is presented in appendix B to estimate the extent to which the estimates are robust to violations of SI. The analysis suggests that the results from the mediation analysis are somewhat sensitive to violations of SI.

included in the analysis to account for potential confounding effects. Descriptive statistics for all of the variables used in the analysis are presented in table A.4.

Results
Results from the mediation analysis are presented in table A.5 and subsequently described.

Students Are More Likely to Learn Math When Their Teacher Is Frequently Monitored by the School Principal
The principal monitoring index variable has a positive and statistically significant indirect effect on student math outcomes that is mediated through teachers' effort in providing feedback to students and creating an environment of respect and rapport. In other words, teachers are more likely to put forth more effort in their teaching when frequently monitored by principals, and students tend to learn better when taught by teachers who exert higher levels of effort.

Specifically, as mediated by teachers' effort in providing feedback to students, increasing principal monitoring from an index of 2—at the bottom of the distribution—to an index of 11—at the top of the distribution—may increase student outcomes by an average of roughly 0.03 SD in math test scores that are prone to memorization, and, more importantly, by approximately 0.02 SD in math scores that are suggestive of actual student learning. Similarly, when considered through teachers' effort in creating an environment of respect and rapport, the indirect effect of principal monitoring may be as high as 0.05 SD in math test scores that are suggestive of actual student learning, for an increase in 9 points in the principal monitoring index.

Students Are Also More Likely to Learn Language Skills When Their Teacher Is Frequently Monitored by the School Principal
The indirect effect of principal monitoring on students' language outcomes is no different than in mathematics. Increasing principal monitoring from an index of 2—at the bottom of the distribution—to an index of 11—at the top of the

distribution—may increase student outcomes by an average of roughly 0.05 SD in language test scores that are prone to memorization, and by approximately 0.04 SD in language scores that are suggestive of actual student learning—as mediated by teachers' effort in providing feedback to students. Furthermore, the indirect effect of principal monitoring, when mediated by teachers' effort in creating an environment of respect and rapport, may be as high as 0.07 SD in language test scores that are suggestive of actual student learning, for an increase in 9 points in the index.

As expected, with principal monitoring having a very weak effect on teachers' effort in areas that are difficult to observe, the principal monitoring index has a statically significant indirect effect on only one of the student outcome measures (reading comprehension) that is mediated through teachers' effort in designing student assessments. Furthermore, the index has no statistically significant indirect effect on any of the four measures of student outcomes, mediated through teachers' effort in designing coherent instruction.[7]

Comparative Case Study in Jordanian Schools

The results of the empirical analyses in the "Principal Monitoring and Teacher Effort" and the "Monitoring, Teacher Effort, and Student Learning in Jordan" sections suggest that teachers are more likely to put forth effort in their teaching (in areas where effort is observable) when they are closely monitored by their principals. Moreover, the mediation analysis suggests that principal monitoring is positively associated with student learning, as mediated by teacher effort. Although the results are consistent with expectations, they are also vulnerable to endogeneity concerns and the potential of omitted variable bias. As the principal monitoring variable is constructed using observational data—and thus not randomly assigned—it is likely that it is correlated with unobservable factors that also influence teacher effort and student learning. If this index is indeed correlated with such unobservable factors, then the estimates in the previous two sections cannot be interpreted causally, and are rather associations.

Aiming to gain insight into relevant causal mechanisms that could potentially add inferential leverage to the quantitative analyses in the previous sections, a comparative case study of six Jordanian schools was conducted using statistical matching for the case selection, followed by a process-tracing procedure. The results of the comparative case study analysis are highly complementary of the empirical analysis, suggesting that teachers do indeed put forth more effort in their teaching when their principals closely monitor them.

Methodology

To address potential endogeneity concerns, the comparative case study needs to rule out alternative causal mechanisms driving teacher effort. To do so, statistical matching is first used to identify most similar cases, ensuring that the observed levels of teacher effort cannot be attributed to observable characteristics. Then, the remaining empirical variation among the selected cases is dealt with by using process tracing, whereby the causal process by which teacher effort came about is examined within and across selected cases, as described below.

Case Selection through Matching

To guide the selection of cases, Mahalanobis Distance Matching (MDM)—a statistical matching technique that measures the distance between two observations in a set of covariates—is used to identify matched pairs of schools that resemble each other as closely as possible in observable directorate-, school-, teacher-, and student-level characteristics, while varying in the degree to which the principal monitors teachers. Toward this end, a dichotomous variable is created at the school level, taking the value of 1 if a school scores 8 or higher in the principal monitoring index ("high principal monitoring"), or a value of 0 if it scores 7 or lower in this index ("low principal monitoring").[8] Through MDM, schools are then paired together such that each pair comprises a "high principal monitoring" school and a "low principal monitoring" school that are as close as possible in a similarity distance measure based on a vector of covariates that includes school wealth index, households with computer, rural/urban, frequency of school visits by directorate inspector, frequency of classroom visits by directorate supervisor, frequency of parent–teacher association meetings, teacher-student ratio, and teacher educational attainment. This selection procedure produces one school pairing in each region of Jordan (North, Center, and South). Each resulting pair of schools is very similar across the different covariates, while at the same time varying in the principal monitoring index: the first school pairing has a difference of 4 points (9–5) for the index, while the other two school pairings each have a difference of 2 points (8–6). The three paired cases serve as mutual—imperfect— counterfactuals that rule out observable characteristics as confounders of the relationship of interest (Nielsen 2014).

Process-Tracing Procedure

Once the three paired cases are selected, a process-tracing procedure is used to rule out potentially unobserved intervening variables (George and Bennet 2005). Specifically, and as motivated by the literature, potential unobserved variables explored include the presence of teacher incentives that may be attached to principals' monitoring mechanisms, and teacher selection bias—whereby more motivated teachers who exert higher levels of effort self-select into schools headed by more motivated principals who conduct more monitoring. Toward this end, in-depth, semi-structured interviews are conducted with principals and two second or third grade teachers at each selected school, tracing the causal process—if any—from principal monitoring to teacher effort. Within each school pairing, the causal process by which higher teacher effort came about in the "high principal monitoring" school is contrasted against its "low principal monitoring" pair. If a causal relationship is found, the analysis then contemplates whether this relationship is found repeatedly across the three school pairings (Collier 2011).

Results
Principals Seldom Rely on Incentive Mechanisms to Elicit Higher Teacher Effort
The study investigated the presence of both financial and nonfinancial incentives as potential confounders in the relationship between principal monitoring and teacher effort. With regard to the former, every one of the interviewees confirmed the absence of financial incentives at the school level. This is consistent with the fact that, as in most countries where teacher payment is centralized, principals in Jordanian schools have no authority to reward high teacher performance through increased salary or bonuses. Furthermore, when asked about punitive financial incentives, teachers across all selected schools agreed that these, too, were absent. They all mentioned dock in payment as a potential punishment for unexcused absenteeism. Yet, none of them recalled being subject to docked payment or knowing another teacher whose payment had been docked.

Absent financial incentives, principals could resort to nonfinancial rewards and sanctions, over which they have considerable latitude, to elicit higher teacher effort. Yet, out of the six selected schools, only one school principal—in a low principal monitoring pair—was found to systematically recognize her teachers' level of effort by organizing "teacher of the year" contests each academic year. Interviews with teachers at this school, however, revealed their lack of awareness of the criteria used by the principal to award this recognition, with one teacher even questioning "How can the principal recognize [them] at the end of the year if she did not know about [their] daily performance in the classroom?" contrasting this school with its high principal monitoring pair exposes an important teacher effort gap in favor of the high principal monitoring school, suggesting that strong principal monitoring is a prerequisite for nonfinancial recognitions that intend to elicit higher teacher effort. Principal and teacher interviews also revealed that in two schools (one high principal monitoring pair, and one low principal monitoring pair), symbolic gifts—such as the Holy Quran, flowers, thank you cards, or pins—were used at times by principals. In neither case were these gifts tied to teachers' performance, however; rather, they were handed to all teachers as a gesture of appreciation. Teachers expressed their gratitude when asked about these tokens of appreciation, but were also candid in expressing that poor-performing teachers were recognized equally with those who put significantly more effort into teaching. As such, the analysis was not able to trace these gestures of appreciation to teachers' level of effort in either school.

Turning to nonfinancial sanctions, the study found two schools (both high principal monitoring pairs) in which principals attached punitive consequences to their monitoring. These consequences took the form of verbal reprimands in private and in the presence of colleagues as a penalty for underperformance. In contrast to their low principal monitoring pairs, interviewed teachers in these schools were very certain that any underperformance would be noticed and sanctioned by the principal. In one teacher's own words, "The principal observes [their] teaching very often. [They] do not know when she may pay [them] a visit, and if [they] are not prepared she will be strict." This may indicate that increased teacher effort may be a result of principal monitoring and sanctions attached to this monitoring. Yet, a word of caution is in order. Some teachers at these schools condemned the negative environment that these sanctions had created in the school, describing how they affected teacher morale. In this regard, comparing these schools with the third high principal monitoring pair (in which the use of sanctions was not prevalent) suggests that sanctions may actually not be a necessary condition for principal monitoring to elicit higher teacher effort.

Positive Incentives Could Significantly Enhance the Effect of Monitoring on Teacher Effort

A recent strand of literature shows that nonfinancial rewards can be effective in settings where the power of financial incentives is limited (Ashraf, Oriana, and Jack 2014). Certainly, recognizing teachers' effort and achievements can increase their motivation, incentivizing them to keep up the good work or increase their level of effort. Yet, the evidence above suggests that principals in Jordan seldom rely on nonfinancial mechanisms to incentivize teacher effort. And when they do, they make use of mechanisms to sanction instead of reward. This is further corroborated by the two-thirds of interviewed teachers (in both high and low principal monitoring pairs) who expressed a very strong desire to be recognized in any way by the principal for their high effort so as to motivate them to keep working hard. Many even expressed their frustration at times when they overperformed at a particular task but were not recognized. For example, a teacher recalled a time when she prepared an excellent lesson plan and the principal simply signed it and wrote "thank you"—as she had done with all other teachers' lesson plans. Another teacher lamented that while all of her mistakes were always pointed out by the principal in her periodic classroom observations, she was not recognized for all of her good work. This suggests that the use of positive nonfinancial incentives may be a promising strategy—currently underutilized in Jordan—that could enhance the effect of principal monitoring on teacher effort.

Teacher Selection Bias Does Not Seem to Drive Higher Teacher Effort

All interviewed teachers agreed about their limited say on their school assignment. They were appointed by the central ministry to any existing vacancy within their governorate of residence. In most cases, when more than one vacancy was available, they asked to be assigned to the school closest to their home so as to better attend to their family-related obligations. When explicitly asked to select the criteria they used to select the school they currently work at, in all cases they put a priority on proximity to place of residence over school quality and reputation. This was consistent both within and across pairings of schools, suggesting a constraining environment for more motivated teachers to self-select into schools with more motivated principals.

A causal relationship was traced between principal monitoring to teacher effort, as evidenced by teachers in high principal monitoring school pairings constantly referring to the need to prepare their classes very well, given that the principal may visit their classroom at any time. Teachers pointed to the specific areas where principals monitored them, or key tasks for which they are always held accountable. For instance, a teacher emphasized periodic monitoring whereby her principal randomly selected students' copybooks to review the quality of the work and the teacher's feedback to the student, leading her to be particularly meticulous when correcting students' assignments. Another teacher highlighted that her principal quizzed students often to ensure that they fully understood the class, which required her to constantly check up on her students to ensure they followed the material. This pattern was systematically repeated across high principal monitoring school pairings, and seemed significantly weaker—if at all present—in the low principal monitoring pairs. This evidence, together with the weak incentives environment and the constraining environment for teacher self-selection in Jordan, suggests that teachers do indeed put forth more effort in their teaching when their principals closely monitor them.

Conclusions

Overall, the findings of this chapter reveal suboptimal levels of teacher effort across classrooms in Jordan, while underscoring the pivotal role of principals in increasing teacher effort. The results of the empirical analyses suggest that teachers are more likely to put forth effort in their teaching when they are closely monitored by their principals. Specifically, teachers who are frequently monitored are more likely to provide feedback to their students. Similarly, more effort in creating a positive learning environment is put forth by teachers who are monitored more often. Furthermore, the mediation analysis suggests that principal monitoring is positively associated with student learning, as mediated by teacher effort. Increasing principal monitoring from an index of 2—at the bottom of the distribution—to an index of 11—at the top of the distribution—may increase student outcomes by up to 0.07 SD and 0.05 SD in language and math test scores, respectively, on average. Evidence from a comparative case study across six Jordanian schools adds inferential leverage to the quantitative analyses, easing potential endogeneity concerns. Informed by these findings, chapter 4 explores key policy implications for the education sector in Jordan.

Notes

1. Exogenous shocks, namely the recent incorporation of many refugee students into the education system as a result of the ongoing conflict in the Middle East, may have affected the resilience of the education system and with it, education inputs and/or outputs in localized areas. This exogenous shock, with its corresponding inflow of inputs in the form of international aid, occurred after the data used in this study were collected and, thus, are outside the scope of this study.

2. As it would be expected, there is an urban-rural divide, as well as regional variation in class size, ranging from an average class size of 17 in the rural South Region to 31 in the urban Center Region (World Bank 2016).

3. This is the teacher absenteeism rate as reported by school principals, which might be an underestimation of the actual rate, masking excused absences allowed under certain conditions by the principal. Teacher absenteeism rates as measured by external observers through unannounced visits are not available for Jordan.

4. Jordan's Civil Service Bureau stipulates seven specific roles for school principals, against which the latter are evaluated in their Annual Performance Record. These are (1) following up with staff's daily performance, (2) developing and enabling school staff and ensuring the provision of an appropriate learning environment; (3) understanding and complying with the philosophy and core values of the education system; (4) organizing the school council's meetings and activating the engagement of the local community; (5) cooperating with the supervisors to improve the teachers' performance; (6) providing school supplies to ensure effective procedures; and (7) enhancing education concepts and codes of conduct for staff and students.

5. The component measures for the principal monitoring index variable are complements of each other. The complementary relationship between the two component measures ensures that the principal monitoring index variable is a reasonable proxy for the true monitoring environment within a given school.

6. FFT divides the complex activity of teaching into 22 components, clustered into four domains of teaching responsibility: (1) planning and preparation, (2) classroom environment, (3) instruction, and (4) professional responsibilities. Table A.1 presents FFT's four domains and respective components. FFT's fourth domain (Professional Responsibilities) has not been included in this study, as it is aimed to capture teachers' professional development, which this study regards as part of teachers' knowledge frontier, and teachers' effort in outreach activities with the community at large.

7. In terms of the direct effect, the mediation analysis generally suggests that principal monitoring has no direct effect on student outcomes. The principal monitoring index is shown to be positively associated with only one measure of student outcomes (Reading Comprehension). Estimates for the direct effect of principal monitoring on student outcomes are available upon request.

8. The cutoff point is the sample mean for the index ($\bar{x} = 7.22$).

References

Angrist, Joshua, and Victor Lavy. 1999. "Using Maimonides' Rule to Estimate the Effect of Class Size on Scholastic Achievement." *Quarterly Journal of Economics* 114 (2): 533–75.

Ashraf, Nava, Bandiera Oriana, and B. Kelsey Jack. 2014. "No Margin, No Mission? A Field Experiment on Incentives for Public Service Delivery." *Journal of Public Economics* 120: 1–17.

Banerjee, Abhijit V., Shawn Cole, Esther Duflo, and Leigh Linden. 2007. "Remedying Education: Evidence from Two Randomized Experiments in India." *Quarterly Journal of Economics* 122 (3): 1235–64.

Barrera-Osorio, Felipe, and Leigh L. Linden. 2009. "The Use and Misuse of Computers in Education: Evidence from a Randomized Controlled Trial of a Language Arts Program." Working Paper, Columbia University, New York.

Bau, Natalie, and Jishnu Das. 2016. "The Misallocation of Pay and Productivity in the Public Sector: Evidence from the Labor Market for Teachers." Working Paper,

World Bank, Washington, DC. http://pubdocs.worldbank.org/en/27011146618606
6575/contract-teacher-paper-NBau-notreformatted.pdf.

Bornstein, Marc C., and Robert H. Bradley, eds. 2003. *Socioeconomic Status, Parenting, and Child Development*. Mahwah, NJ: Erlbaum.

Branch, G., E. Hanushek, and S. Rivkin. 2013. "School Leaders Matter." *Education Next* 13 (1): 62–69.

Brooks-Gunn, J., and G. J. Duncan. 1997. "The Effects of Poverty on Children." *The Future of Children* 7 (2): 55–71.

Bruns, B., and J. Luque. 2014. *Great Teachers: How to Raise Student Learning in Latin America and the Caribbean*. Washington, DC: World Bank.

Chaudhury, N., J. Hammer, M. Kremer, K. Muralidharan, and H. Rogers. 2005. "Missing in Action: Teacher and Health Worker Absence in Developing Countries." *Journal of Economic Perspectives* 20 (1): 91–116.

Coleman, J. S. 1988. "Social Capital in the Creation of Human Capital." *American Journal of Sociology* 94: S95–120.

Collier, D. 2011. "Understanding Process Tracing." *PS: Political Science and Politics* 44 (4): 823–30.

Cristia, J., P. Ibarrán, S. Cueto, A. Santiago, and E. Severín. 2012. "Technology and Child Development: Evidence from the One Laptop per Child Program." IZA Discussion Paper 6401, Forschungsinstitut zur Zukunft der Arbeit GmbH, Bonn, Germany.

Duflo, E., R. Hanna, and S. Ryan. 2012. "Incentives Work: Getting Teachers to Come to School." *American Economic Review* 102 (4): 1241–78.

Gates Foundation. 2012. "Gathering Feedback for Teaching. Combining High-Quality Observations with Student Surveys and Achievement Gains." MET Project Research Paper.

George, A., and A. Bennet. 2005. *Case Studies and Theory Development in the Social Sciences*. Cambridge, MA: MIT Press.

Glewwe, P., M. Kremer, S. Moulin, and E. Zitzewitz. 2004. "Retrospective vs. Prospective Analyses of School Inputs: The Case of Flip Charts in Kenya." *Journal of Development Economics* 74: 251–68.

Glewwe, P., N. Ilias, and M. Kremer. 2010. "Teacher Incentives." *American Economic Journal: Applied Economics* 2 (3): 205–27.

Hamre, B., and R. Pianta. 2007. "Learning Opportunities in Preschool and Early Elementary Classrooms." In *School Readiness and the Transition to Kindergarten in the Era of Accountability*, edited by R. Pianta, M. Cox, and K. Snow, 49–84. Baltimore, MD: Brookes.

Hanushek, Eric A., and J. Luque. 2003. "Efficiency and Equity in Schools around the World." *Economics of Education Review* 22: 481–502.

Hanushek, Eric A., John F. Kain, Daniel M. O'Brien, and Steven G. Rivkin. 2005. "The Market for Teacher Quality." Working Paper 11154, National Bureau of Economic Research, Cambridge, MA.

Hanushek, E., and S. Rivkin. 2006. "Teacher Quality." In *Handbook of the Economics of Education*, edited by E. Hanushek and F. Welch, 1052–75. Vol. 2. Amsterdam: North Holland.

———. 2010. "Generalizations about Using Value-Added Measures of Teacher Quality." *American Economic Review* 100 (2): 267–71.

Hicks, Raymond, and Dustin Tingley. 2011. "Causal Mediation Analysis." *The Stata Journal* 11 (4): 609–15.

IEA (International Association for the Evaluation of Educational Achievement). 2011. "Trends in International Mathematics and Science Study 2011 Results: Jordan Country Profile." IEA, Boston, MA.

Imai, Kosuke, Luke Keele, and Dustin Tingley. 2010. "A General Approach to Causal Mediation Analysis." *Psychological Methods* 15 (4): 309–34.

Imberman, Scott. 2011. "The Effect of Charter Schools on Achievement and Behavior of Public School Students." *Journal of Public Economics* 95 (7–8): 850–63.

Kane, Thomas J. 2004. "The Impact of After-School Programs: Interpreting the Results of Four Recent Evaluations." Working Paper of the William T. Grant Foundation, New York.

Kane, Thomas J., Jonah E. Rockoff, and Douglas O. Staiger. 2006. "What Does Certification Tell Us about Teacher Effectiveness? Evidence from New York City." NBER Working Paper 12155, National Bureau of Economic Research, Cambridge, MA.

Kane, Thomas J., and Douglas O. Staiger. 2008. "Estimating Teacher Impacts on Student Achievement: An Experimental Evaluation." NBER Working Paper 14607, National Bureau of Economic Research, Cambridge, MA.

Krueger, A. 1999. "Experimental Estimates of Education Production Functions." *Quarterly Journal of Economics* 114 (2): 497–532.

Krueger, Alan B., and Diane M. Whitmore. 2001. "The Effect of Attending a Small Class in the Early Grades on College-Test Taking and Middle School Test Results: Evidence from Project STAR." *The Economic Journal* 111 (468): 1–28.

Lavy, V., M. D. Paserman, and A. Schlasser. 2011. "Inside the Black Box of Ability Peer Effects: Evidence from Variation in the Proportion of Low Achievers in the Classroom." *The Economic Journal* 122 (559): 208–337.

Muralidharan, Karthik, and Venkatesh Sundararaman. 2011. "Teacher Performance Pay: Experimental Evidence from India." *Journal of Political Economy* 119 (1): 39–77.

Nielsen, Richard A. 2014. "Case Selection via Matching." *Sociological Methods & Research* 45 (3). doi:10.1177/0049124114547054.

Nye, Barbara, Spyros Konstantopoulos, and Larry V. Hedges. 2004. "How Large Are Teacher Effects?" *Educational Evaluation and Policy Analysis* 26 (3): 237–57.

OECD (Organisation for Economic Co-operation and Development). 2012. "Programme for International Student Assessment 2012 Results: Jordan Country Profile." OECD, Paris.

RAND. 2012. *Teachers Matter: Understanding Teachers' Impact on Student Achievement.* Santa Monica, CA: RAND Corporation.

Sirin, S. 2005. "Socioeconomic Status and Academic Achievement: A Meta-analytic Review of Research." *Review of Educational Research* 75 (3): 417–53.

Stallings, J. A. 1986. "Effective Use of Time in Secondary Reading Programs." In *Effective Teaching of Reading: Research and Practice*, edited by J. Hoffman, 85–106. Newark, DE: International Reading Association.

Urquiola, M. 2006. "Identifying Class Size Effects in Developing Countries: Evidence from Rural Bolivia." *The Review of Economics and Statistics* 88 (1): 171–77.

USAID (United States Agency for International Development). 2012. *Student Performance in Reading and Mathematics, Pedagogic Practice, and School Management in Jordan.* EdData II Technical and Managerial Assistance Report. Washington, DC: USAID.

World Bank. 2010. *Saber Country Report: Teachers; Kingdom of Jordan.* Washington, DC: World Bank.

———. 2012. *World Development Indicators Data.* Washington, DC: World Bank.

———. 2015. *World Development Indicators Data.* Washington, DC: World Bank.

———. 2016. "Jordan Education Public Expenditure Review: Background Analysis." World Bank, Washington, DC.

CHAPTER 3

Healthcare Quality, Provider Effort, and Accountability

Introduction

An enormous academic and policy-focused literature has sought to identify and evaluate the inputs that affect the quality of healthcare service provision. This literature can be divided into research that analyzes the (1) structural and (2) behavioral determinants of healthcare provision (Das and Hammer 2014).

Structural determinants include factors that can readily be addressed with increased funding, such as the physical condition and availability of medical facilities, the quality of equipment, and the amount of medicine on shelves. Even the number of staff and the caseload for individual providers are structural determinants. It would seem reasonable to believe that in developing countries structural determinants would be the far more important factor in improving healthcare provision. In fact, the international community has focused largely on improving these structural inputs (Das and Hammer 2014) with a specific emphasis on improving the availability of healthcare in developing countries (Das and Gertler 2007). Evidence suggests that these structural factors are not the most important in improving healthcare service provision in these countries, however.

Even in very low-income countries, the equipment necessary to treat common health conditions seems to be abundantly available and does not pose an obstacle for healthcare service delivery (Das and Gertler 2007). A review of healthcare impact evaluations in developing countries finds no correlation between structural inputs and quality (Das and Hammer 2014). Furthermore, while medical education, or lack thereof, is an important structural feature that is highly correlated with having the knowledge to correctly treat patients, improving the knowledge of medical providers may ultimately have minimal effect on improving patient outcomes. This is because the amount of effort exerted by providers is alarmingly low in many contexts (Das and Hammer 2014). Thus, while a lack of medical knowledge hinders the provision of high-quality care, it does not seem to be the main hindrance.[1] Even when providers have the knowledge to correctly treat a patient, they very often fail to do so, which is not the result of a lack of other structural inputs, but rather a result of behavioral determinants.

Behavioral determinants are factors that describe what health providers do within a given level of structural determinants. This incorporates a number of different aspects, from the most basic, such as whether providers consistently show up to work on time, to the most critical, relating to providers' use of knowledge to correctly diagnose and prescribe for patients. Most research has found that these behaviors are seldom practiced, underscoring a lack of effort on the part of healthcare providers to meet expected performance standards.

Healthcare Provider Effort

Just as in the previous chapter on education, absenteeism is a straightforward manifestation of low provider effort. Notwithstanding provider knowledge or even the availability of high-tech equipment, if a health provider fails to show up to work, there is no chance to improve patient outcomes. Furthermore, just as in the case of education, absenteeism is a chronic problem in many developing countries.

In a study carried out in six countries across multiple developing regions, Chaudhury and others (2006) find that, on average, 35 percent of health workers were not present during unannounced visits to health facilities. Banerjee, Deaton, and Duflo (2004) find that 36 percent of providers were absent on an average day in the larger urban healthcare centers in Rajasthan, India, and note an even higher absenteeism rate of 45 percent in smaller rural facilities. The latter is particularly problematic since many small rural centers have only one provider so when s/he fails to show up to work, the clinic simply does not open. Callen and others (2013) find an even higher absenteeism rate of 68.5 percent prior to a randomized intervention in Pakistani health centers. Banerjee, Duflo, and Glennerster (2008) find that the majority of rural government health centers were closed more often than not because the attending nurse failed to report to work.

These figures are consistently higher than those reported for teachers (Chaudhury and others 2006). One explanation may be that healthcare providers have greater alternative options for income. Chaudhury and others (2006) find that the only consistent predictor of provider absence is type of health worker: doctors have higher absence rates than less qualified healthcare professionals (for example, nurses) in all six countries in the study, as doctors have more lucrative options moonlighting at private facilities. For example, in Peru, 48 percent of doctors reported earning extra income in private facilities whereas only 30 percent of other health professionals reported outside income. When doctors have the opportunity to moonlight, they devote less time to patients and have higher rates of absenteeism in public sector facilities (Ferrinho and others 2004).

While absenteeism is clearly a major problem that results from lack of provider effort as opposed to inadequate structural inputs, the fact is that even when providers do show up to work they often fail to exert substantial effort. Providers frequently do not follow basic clinical practice guidelines (CPGs) (that is, taking patient history, physical examinations, test ordering, diagnosis, and treatment), spend inadequate amounts of time with patients, and do not maximize the value of their medical training in interactions with patients. Studies have found that providers spend remarkably little time with patients even in facilities with high levels of excess capacity. For example, the average consultation time in urban and rural India is three minutes. Furthermore, providers average only three questions per consultation. One-third of consultations are over in less than a minute and only involve the question "What's wrong with you?" (Das, Hammer, and Leonard 2008). The same study finds similar figures in several other low-income countries. In contrast, the average consultation time in an Organisation for Economic Co-operation and Development (OECD) country is three to four times longer (Das and Hammer 2014).

A "know-do" gap in the provision of healthcare has been found in a number of studies on healthcare provision in the developing world: for example, by Das and Hammer (2007) in the context of India, Leonard, Masatu, and Vialou (2007) in Tanzania, and Gertler and Vermeersch (2012) in Rwanda. In all of these studies, researchers have found that providers often have sufficient knowledge to address common medical problems, and yet fail to do so when they interact with real patients. Essentially, providers fail to exert the effort necessary to utilize their medical training.

The earlier discussed finding that absenteeism rates are higher in public hospitals carries over to the levels of effort exerted even when providers are present: providers exert less effort at public healthcare centers than at private ones. Das and Hammer (2007) find that providers spend 30–50 percent less time with patients in public healthcare centers than in private ones. Das and others (2013) compare private and public clinics in the Indian state of Madhya Pradesh and find that providers spend longer amounts of time in consultation, ask more questions, and perform more exams at private clinics than at public clinics. The results hold even for the same provider who spends time working at both public and private clinics. This result indicates that providers expend less effort at public healthcare facilities because fewer performance-based incentives exist in public facilities. This is not a function of structural disadvantages at public facilities. In fact, in the Das and others (2013) study, the authors show that excess capacity exists in both private and public facilities and that public facilities have better equipment than private facilities.

None of these indicators of low provider effort can be easily explained by heavy caseloads for providers either. If this were the case, it might be optimal for providers to exert low levels of effort so as to conserve energy and/or time to see a larger number of patients. However, the evidence does not support this idea. Studies have found large excess capacity in public clinics in Tanzania, Senegal, Kenya, and India (Das and Hammer 2014).[2] Researchers found that providers rarely see more than 15 patients per day and on average spend 40 minutes per day with patients. Instead, providers do not exert effort because they are not incentivized to do so. If providers do not exert effort then improving structural determinants of healthcare provision is unlikely to improve patient outcomes. Thus, improving provider effort is key to improving healthcare provision. To do this, the most promising avenue is to increase provider accountability.

The Last Mile to Quality Service Delivery in Jordan • http://dx.doi.org/10.1596/978-1-4648-1069-5

Holding Healthcare Providers Accountable to Increase Provider Effort
The evidence clearly indicates that lack of provider effort is a common problem and that this is likely more important than many, if not all, structural factors that are often the focus of international interventions. As such, researchers have spent substantial time analyzing the best methods of improving provider effort. Nearly all of these methods involve increasing the accountability of providers. The rationale is that the lack of effort is a function of systems that do not incentivize effort because providers are compensated regardless of effort levels. Essentially, providers are not accountable for their performance and so choose to expend less effort.

Thus, it may be expected that increasing accountability will increase provider effort. As discussed in previous chapters, improving accountability requires monitoring and incentivizing high levels of effort. Also, as discussed previously, issues of "observability" and "farther outcome" emerge when trying to monitor and properly incentivize effort.

The Observability Challenge
Making providers accountable necessitates being able to observe and evaluate provider effort. Provider effort can be divided into two categories: effort to attend work and effort in interactions with patients. To ensure provider accountability, both aspects of provider effort must be observable.

Monitoring of provider absenteeism can be implemented using a top-down, bottom-up, or within-facility approach.

A common top-down method of observing provider absenteeism is for governments to employ inspectors to randomly visit health centers and check for provider presence (Callen and others 2013). This type of top-down approach has proven to be difficult in practice. A number of studies find that providers are able to pressure inspectors into giving favorable reviews even when they are absent when the inspector shows up (Banerjee and Duflo 2006; Callen and others 2013). Essentially, this means that the inspector covers for deficiencies in provider performance (Banerjee and Duflo 2006). Callen and others (2013) also find that external party control by government inspectors often fails because providers have political connections that they use to pressure inspectors.

Bottom-up approaches often involve forming community organizations that monitor provider absenteeism through direct observation (that is, random or regular checks at provider facilities) or through patient complaints (Banerjee, Deaton, and Duflo 2004; Banerjee and Duflo 2006). This method has had varying levels of success according to impact evaluations. The reason for the varied outcomes seems to be that monitoring by local communities is subject to a severe collective action issue. The community would like to monitor and enforce high levels of provider effort, but each individual in the community would be better off if someone else did the work necessary to monitor and enforce (Banerjee and Duflo 2006). In Banerjee, Deaton, and Duflo (2004), individuals from the local community were paid to randomly check on whether providers were present at their assigned health center. The study found that local monitoring had no effect on provider absenteeism because the community was either unable or unwilling to create an enforcement mechanism. Björkman and Svensson (2010) find that factors that reduce the ability of a community to collectively organize (such as income inequality and ethnic fractionalization) reduce the effectiveness of community-based monitoring.

Within-facility monitoring of provider absenteeism occurs when a supervisor of a facility, often the chief medical officer (CMO), observes provider absenteeism. Mechanisms of promoting provider effort within facilities deserve more attention than they have received thus far in development research and may address some of the limitations of top-down and bottom-up accountability. An emphasis on within-facility accountability capitalizes on the technical knowledge of supervisors within health centers. This approach, as well as the other two mentioned above, has the ability to observe provider absenteeism if implemented properly.

The "observability" challenge really emerges in the monitoring of provider effort in consultations with patients. As discussed in the prior section, ample evidence shows that providers do not exert high levels of effort when interacting with patients. To make providers accountable for failing to exert effort, it is necessary to observe them interacting with patients. However, observing patient-provider interactions is inherently problematic because of the private nature of the interactions. Using a top-down approach to observe this would require an outside party, perhaps the same government inspector that monitors attendance, to be present in such interactions. This clearly breeches privacy, considered one of the primary components of rights-based healthcare provision (Leonard and Masatu 2006).

One means of overcoming this problem is to use patient surveys after provider service to evaluate the effort of providers—a form of bottom-up monitoring. This would not violate privacy as patients could choose whether to respond; they would not need to disclose personal medical information while still providing insight into their provider's effort and overall performance. Unfortunately, patients do not appear capable of evaluating provider service. Banerjee and Duflo (2006) find that survey respondents reported that their last visit to healthcare centers made them feel better despite the extremely low levels of provider effort measured at the same healthcare centers. Similarly, Das and Sanchez-Paramo (2004) find large-N survey evidence indicating that individuals have essentially no ability to identify sources of quality care. Banerjee, Deaton, and Duflo (2004) suggest that patients may have a limited ability to evaluate provider service because of extremely low expectations. If patients are used to low levels of provider effort, then they will view low-effort providers as the norm.

Lastly, supervisors within health centers can act as monitors. A CMO within a health center should have the knowledge to act as an effective monitor and not be subject to the same privacy issues associated with top-down monitoring.

The Farther Outcome Problem

In the context of healthcare provision, the "farther outcome" challenge relates to the difficulty in directly evaluating provider performance and being forced to evaluate providers based on other measures. Essentially, because of the "observability" challenge discussed in the prior section, evaluating provider effort must be based on outcomes other than actually observing the provider at work. This creates challenges in the measurement and choice of outcomes to be evaluated.

In the case of absenteeism, measurement is not an issue; measuring whether a provider reports to work should be a simple process. However, measuring a provider's performance while at work is a much more difficult task. We can think of there being two types of common evaluation methods: a top-down approach that focuses on health outcomes in a community and a bottom-up approach that focuses on patient surveys.

A top-down approach would be to evaluate provider performance on health outcomes in the community where the provider is located. For example, providers could be evaluated on the prevalence of illness or under-5 mortality rates in the community. The two problems with this type of evaluation are both related to the "farther outcome" problem. First, a host of factors unrelated to provider performance affect health outcomes in the community where the provider works. For example, Marmot and Wilkinson (2005) detail the importance of socioeconomic factors in determining health outcomes across societies. These factors include obvious ones such as average incomes in a local community, but also factors such as ethnic diversity and type of housing in a community. Because of the importance of these factors it becomes difficult if not impossible to accurately evaluate performance on health outcomes in the communities where they work. The second issue with evaluation based on health outcomes is choosing which health indicators by which to evaluate providers. For example, if providers know that they are only evaluated on under-5 mortality rates, they may be incentivized to inefficiently allocate their resources to improving this outcome at the cost of a community's overall health.

A bottom-up approach to measuring provider performance would be to evaluate providers based on patient reports. Essentially, provider performance could be judged by satisfaction surveys. This is problematic because of patients' limited ability to evaluate provider performance as discussed in the last section. Of particular relevance to the "farther outcome" challenge is that patients often desire treatments that are not in their own best interest. For example, Banerjee and Duflo (2006) report that patients in India preferred private providers because they were more likely to prescribe shots instead of pills. This was most likely true; government protocol recommends the use of pills when possible, as they are believed to be safer and more cost-effective. However, patients believed that pills were somehow inferior to shots. If providers are evaluated on patient satisfaction, then providers will be incentivized to satisfy patients with treatments that are not in the patient's best interest. Das and Hammer (2014) find evidence of this in India, where providers prescribe an average of three different types of medicine in each consultation. It seems very unlikely that this is optimal. Instead providers appear to be trying to satisfy patients while not exerting effort (this same study found an average consultation time of three minutes and three questions per patient).

Lastly, within-facility approaches can be used to measure provider performance. This approach can potentially solve some, though not all, of the "farther outcome" problems in both top-down and bottom-up approaches. Within facility evaluators will have more knowledge of healthcare provision than patients, thus overcoming some of the problems with bottom-up evaluation. Furthermore, within-facility evaluators should have knowledge of the local communities where providers operate and so be better able to judge which health indicators in a community are attributable to provider performance and which ones are not. Therefore, while within-facility accountability mechanisms cannot solve all issues related to the "farther outcome" problem, within-facility mechanisms should be able to address the issues in ways that top-down and bottom-up approaches cannot.

The Role of CMOs

The literature on improving levels of effort among providers has thus far focused on the role of inspectors and patients as the source of monitoring and evaluation of providers. In contrast, far less research has been conducted on the role of CMOs, who should be in a unique position to observe and evaluate providers. Unlike government inspectors and patients, CMOs have the professional knowledge to evaluate quality in providers. They should be better prepared to overcome the "farther outcome" challenge because of their knowledge of medicine, the specific providers, and local patients.

Furthermore, CMOs are proximate to providers. Rather than relying on random inspections, CMOs are able to monitor providers on a much more regular basis, which helps to overcome the "observability challenge." If nothing else, having a CMO who is regularly present and properly trained to evaluate provider performance should lead to a much larger Hawthorne effect (improved performance simply from being observed) than sporadic observation from either inspectors or patients who are unable to evaluate quality healthcare provision.

In addition CMOs are often evaluated on the performance of providers under their supervision. Thus, part of their existing job description is to monitor and evaluate provider performance. Therefore, they should be among the first avenues of research on improving healthcare provision.

Roadmap to the Chapter

This study is the first nationally representative study in Jordan to measure within-facility accountability and provider effort in primary healthcare facilities and is the first study in the MENA region to investigate the linkages between within-facility accountability and provider efforts, thereby providing novel policy-relevant information on the accountability mechanisms and their drivers that contribute to good service delivery outcomes.

The study in this chapter specifically provides new evidence on the role of CMOs in improving accountability. The "Health Sector in Jordan" section provides an overview of Jordan's health system that indicates the value of focusing on provider effort to improve health outcomes in the country. The "CMO Monitoring and Provider Effort" section uses evidence from a nationally representative sample of 122 primary healthcare centers (PHCCs) representing each of the 13 Directorates of Health in Jordan to test the association between CMO[3] monitoring and provider effort. "Administration of the Instruments" section offers some conclusions.

The Health Sector in Jordan

Jordan enjoys an advanced health system, with one of the most modern healthcare infrastructures in the MENA region, providing a range of both advanced medical services and basic primary care to most citizens at comparatively low direct costs. Over the past two decades, the country has achieved remarkable progress in improving the health status of the population. Life expectancy at birth increased from 69.9 years in 1990 to 73.7 years in 2012; maternal mortality declined from 86 per 100,000 live births in 1990 to 50 in 2013; infant mortality reduced from 34 per 1,000 live births in 1990 to 17 in 2012; and under-5 mortality declined from 39 per 1,000 live births to 21 in the same time period. With these improvements, particularly in maternal and child health, Jordan fares better than many other countries of similar income level, both within and outside of the MENA region (figures 3.1, 3.2, and 3.3). Despite these gains, Jordan's health indicators, especially infant and maternal mortality, suggest that considerable health gains can be made relative to the investment. And since Jordan has reached almost universal coverage in terms of antenatal care, births attended by a skilled health professional, and child immunization, the problem is not one of access but quality of services.

Despite achievements in population health, like many countries of similar economies, Jordan is experiencing an epidemiological transition with a shift from a prevalence of communicable to noncommunicable diseases (NCDs). Three out of every four deaths in Jordan are caused by NCDs (World Health Organization 2011), with cardiovascular and circulatory diseases the leading causes, accounting for about 37 percent of all deaths (IHME 2010). Cancers are the second leading cause of mortality in Jordan, having increased from 9 percent in 1990 to 15 percent of all-cause mortality in 2010 (IHME 2010). Diabetes has secured the third position as a leading cause of death in Jordan, responsible for 7 percent of all deaths in 2010 compared to 2 percent in 1990. Furthermore, the top five conditions associated with the highest disability adjusted life years (DALYs)—a standard measure of morbidity—are related to NCDs. While Jordan's young population composition offers a unique opportunity to capitalize on the potential benefits of the so-called demographic dividend, banking on this for future economic productivity may prove to be a remote possibility if NCDs remain unaddressed.

Addressing the NCD burden in Jordan requires a revitalized focus on primary healthcare while making use of readily available, cost-effective interventions that rely on inexpensive technologies for early detection and diagnosis

Figure 3.1 Life Expectancy: Jordan, MENA Average, and Selected Other Countries, 1980–2011

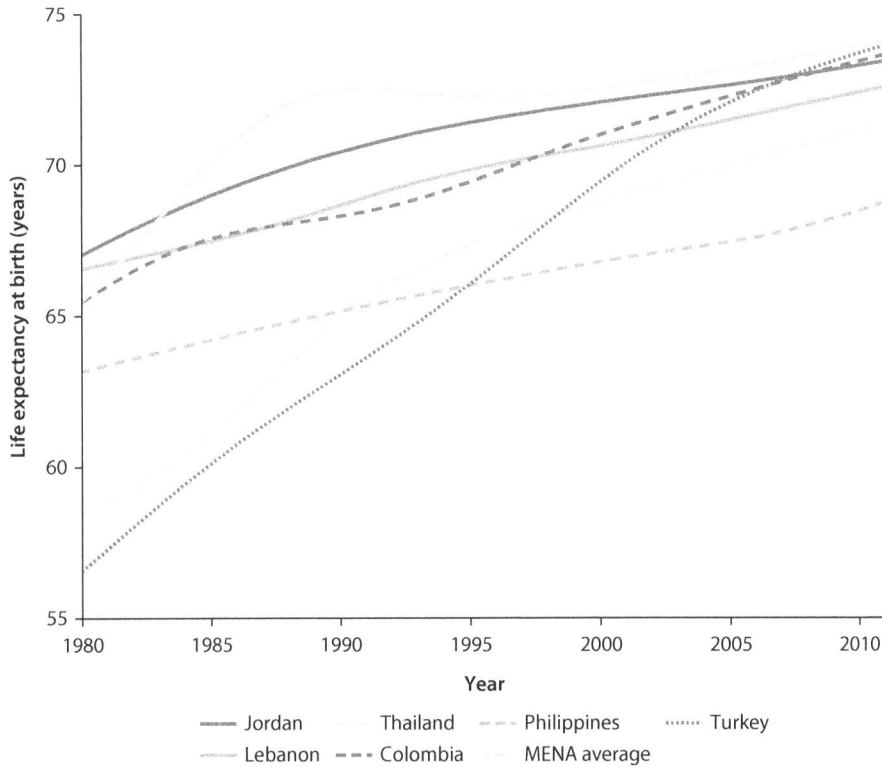

Sources: High Health Council 2013; World Bank 2014; World Health Organization 2014.

(World Health Organization 2010b). International evidence on effective health systems and their ability to promote health, prevent diseases, and manage chronic diseases show that such activities are most cost-effectively performed at the level of communities through primary healthcare. To address the emerging NCD challenge in Jordan, such reorientation would at its core need to uphold primary, and to a lesser degree secondary, prevention strategies that assume a life-course approach (Demaio and others 2014). It would need to ensure that service delivery is both patient-centered and community-based, and would need to be anchored in an environment conducive for delivering services of the highest quality.

Jordan's apparent public health system challenges—particularly as they relate to quality of primary healthcare service delivery—generate a sense of mistrust in the health system on the part of the general public. While limited systematic evidence exists on the quality of healthcare in the country, a number of studies have pointed to perceived deficiencies in the level of primary and hospital care (Abu-Kharmeh 2012; Al-Qutob and Nasir 2008; Khatatbeh 2013; Khoury and Mawajdeh 2004; Otoom and others 2002), which oftentimes is also predicated

Figure 3.2 Infant Mortality versus Income and Total Health Spending, 2011

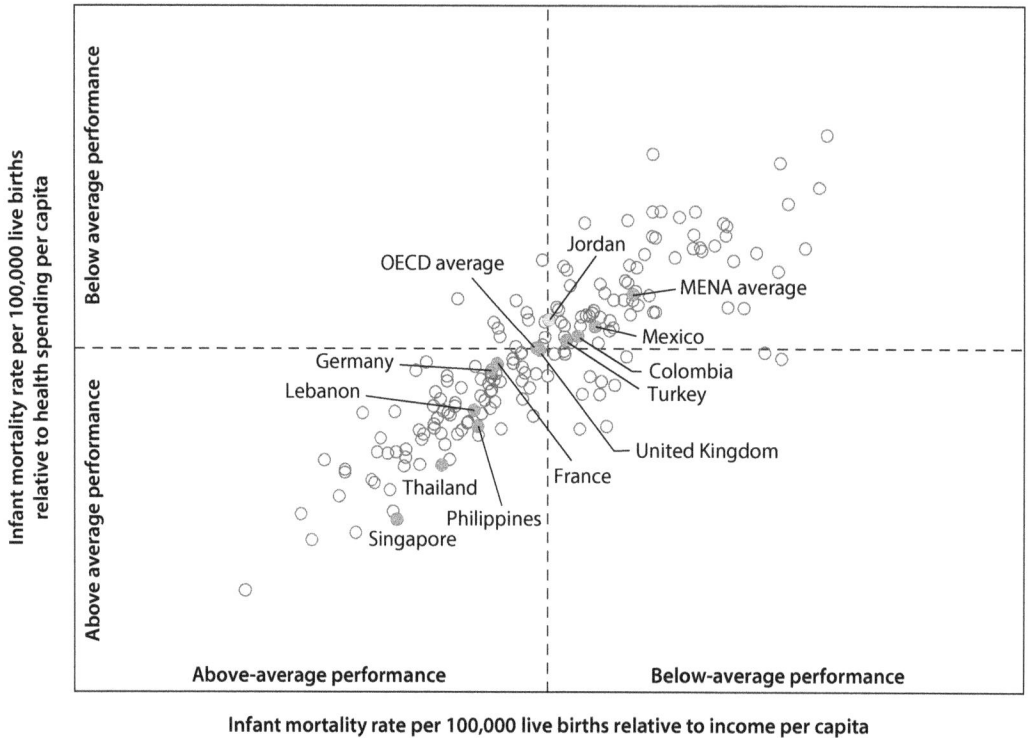

Infant mortality rate per 100,000 live births relative to income per capita

Sources: World Bank 2014; World Health Organization 2014.
Note: Both axes are in log scale.

by geographical factors (Abu-Kharmeh 2012). Drivers for such quality seem to be related to a number of factors, some of which are concomitant with provider effort (Khoury and Mawajdeh 2004; Otoom and others 2002), with one study finding that providers spend less than 30 percent of their clinic time directly providing care (Khoury and Mawajdeh 2004). Other drivers are inherently associated with managerial and supervisory performance (Al-Qutob and Nasir 2008) and, also to a large extent, the incentive environment in which providers operate (Khatatbeh 2013). It has been suggested that the latter two, in the absence of a merit-based system, have mostly resulted in high attrition rates and in many cases replacement with inexperienced providers—especially in rural settings—further impeding the quality of healthcare service delivery (Al-Qutob and Nasir 2008).

While it may be concluded that the underlying dynamics for the perceived inadequate quality of services in Jordan are fueled by limited resources going into the system, the evidence suggests otherwise. In 2011, Jordan's public spending on health as percentage of gross domestic product (GDP) stood at approximately 6 percent, almost double that of the MENA average. This was mirrored in per capita health expenditures, which stood at US$392, well above the averages for

Figure 3.3 Maternal Mortality Relative to Income and Spending, 2010

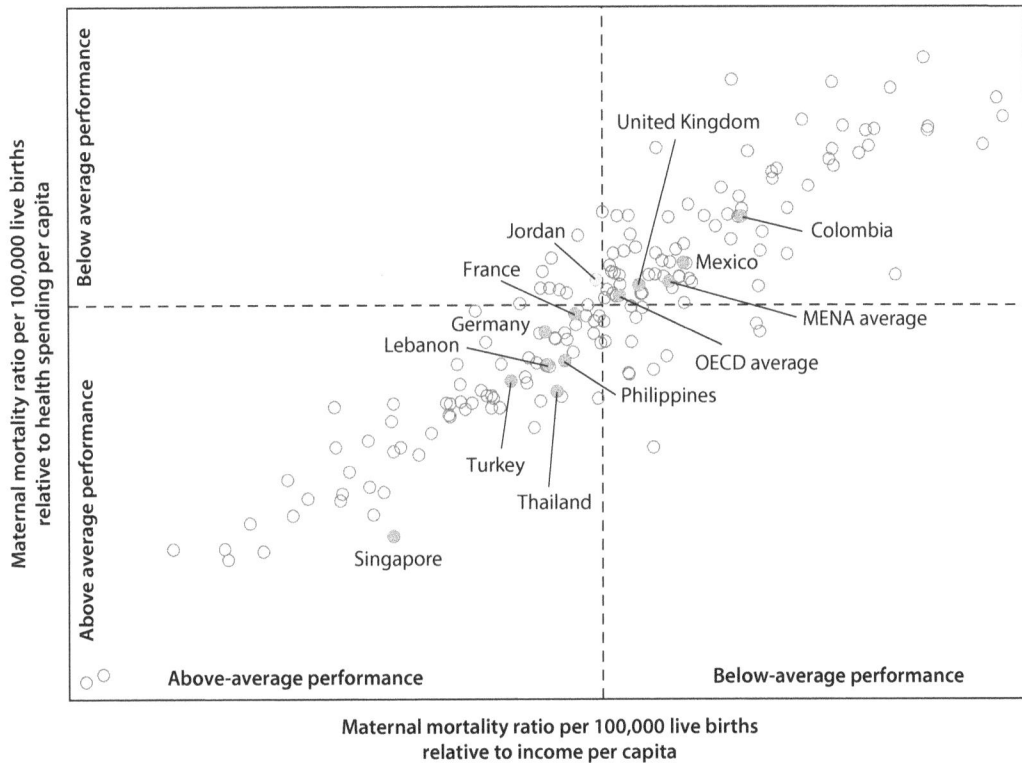

Sources: World Bank 2014; World Health Organization 2014.
Note: Both axes are in log scale.

low- and middle-income countries and for developing countries in the MENA region, although not the highest in the region. Jordan stands out within the region and among countries of similar economies more generally for its high levels of public health spending (figure 3.4).

Jordan's high spending on healthcare implies that the quality production function is not constrained by structural inputs, but rather by a limitation in practice. Whether this is related to provider knowledge or effort, the bottom line is that it is not about investing more in health, but rather addressing the core issues around what actually happens within healthcare settings; that is, at the point of service where patient care is provided. Against this backdrop, it seems that Jordan has hit its input frontier, at least with respect to the large-scale allocation of financial resources to the system. Healthcare professionals are at the frontline of improving the quality of primary care. Designing and implementing programs to boost their commitment and effort can help to advance healthcare quality in Jordan without the allocation of large budget outlays.

With the above said, the promotion of high-quality healthcare is not a new focus for Jordan, and recent initiatives attest that the government and nongovernmental

Figure 3.4 Total Health Expenditure as a Share of GDP and Income Per Capita, 2011

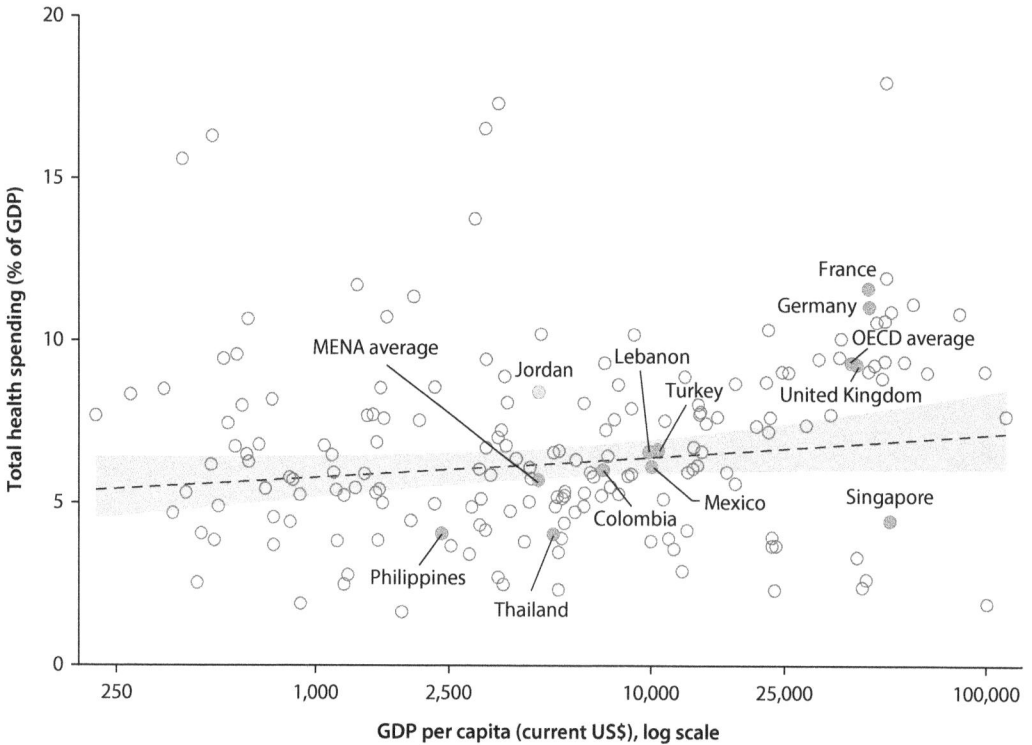

Sources: World Bank 2014; World Health Organization 2014 (3, 5).
Note: x-axis is in log scale.

partners are aware of the importance of human resource management, among other factors, for improving healthcare quality. The Jordan Healthcare Accreditation Program (JHAP) is the most significant recent program adopted by the Jordanian government, in cooperation with international and local partners, to promote quality improvements in the health sector. Initiated in June 2007 and officially completed in March 2013, the JHAP established the Healthcare Accreditation Council (HCAC), an independent, not-for-profit national accreditation agency for the health sector, and, in conjunction with the HCAC, created the National Quality and Safety Goals (NQSG) initiative in Jordan.

The HCAC developed a comprehensive set of standards for healthcare facilities seeking accreditation. These relate to community integration to assess community needs and partner with the community to meet these needs; management and leadership; information and records management; a variety of technical and nontechnical dimensions of the provision of care; the health education of clients and their families; patient safety; environmental safety, infection control, and employee health; and human resource management (Health Care Accreditation Council 2011).

The accreditation program in Jordan has brought about some clear improvements in the primary health system thus far, even if many of its effects have yet to be assessed systematically. Findings from qualitative research on primary health centers in Jordan suggest that the mere preparation for accreditation results in substantive quality improvements such as better medical recordkeeping, more effective human resource management practices, and improved oversight of equipment and consumables, among other outcomes (Rabie, Ekman, and Özçelik 2014). Accreditation appears to have catalyzed increased community input and engagement with local health facilities (Rabie, Ekman, and Özçelik 2014), which in part derives from the requirement for healthcare facilities to establish community health committees (CHCs) to engage with community members and groups more extensively as part of the process (HCAC 2011). The durability of community participation, however, remains to be seen.

Despite Jordan's efforts to promote quality healthcare through the accreditation program and other initiatives, certain features of the health system limit the effectiveness of efforts to improve quality. For example, the system of recruitment, pay, and licensing fosters low quality in primary health centers while the use of public health facilities as the entry point for doctors trained abroad leads to lower-qualified staff and high turnover, as doctors leave public clinics after a short period to return to specialized medical training. Moreover, the large difference in compensation rates across the private and public sectors reduces the incentive for public service, results in high turnover, and encourages dual practice. And the lack of requirements regarding relicensing and the receipt of continuing education threatens the provision of high-quality, evidence-based care.

To further strengthen Jordan's quality of primary healthcare services, serious considerations to quality processes beyond accreditation need to be taken into account, with heightened focus on enhancing provider effort and accountability.

CMO Monitoring and Provider Effort

Is Stronger CMO Monitoring Associated with Higher Provider Effort?

This study was designed to generate knowledge of the relationship between within-facility accountability and provider effort. Specifically, the study seeks to answer whether in a nationally representative sample of PHCCs CMOs' use of accountability mechanisms, namely monitoring practices and incentives, is linked to increased provider effort. The unit of the analysis in the study is the PHCC. Within each PHCC in the sample, data were collected from patients, the CMO, doctors and nurses who work at the center, and, where available, a representative of the CHC. Phone interviews were also conducted with the Head of the Directorate of Health. Findings from this study show variability in provider effort across PHCCs, but consistently high rights-based practice. In general, within-facility accountability mechanisms are characterized by high CMO monitoring coupled with limited nonfinancial rewards, nearly non-existent financial rewards, and uniformity in the application of sanctions. The study also shows that CMO monitoring is highly correlated with high levels of provider effort but not with absenteeism. Finally, in a high sanctions environment, monitoring seems to be associated with greater provision of rights-based care.

Study Sample
The objective of the sampling strategy was to obtain a nationally representative sample of public primary health facilities from all 13 Directorates of Health. The Directorates of Health closely correspond to the 12 governorates in Jordan with the exception of the Governorate of Irbid, which has two directorates. Sample size calculations used to estimate the number of patients and centers required to answer the research question are summarized in appendix C. In summary, the study estimated that a sample size of approximately 120 PHCCs, and 25 patients per PHCC, across all 13 Directorates of Health was needed to test the research question.

The PHCC sample was chosen to be representative of all centers with average daily utilization of at least 35 patients using probability proportionate to the district population size, stratified by the Directorate of Health to ensure representation from all directorates. Study resources allowed only a one-day visit to each center. Therefore, health centers needed to have an average daily utilization of 35 or more patients per day to be included in the sample so that 25 patients could be interviewed, assuming that some patients would be ineligible, too unwell, or unwilling to participate. One Directorate of Health, Tafileh, did not have a PHCC that met the average daily utilization minimum. To ensure representation of that Directorate of Health, one of the two clinics in Tafileh with the highest utilization was randomly chosen. In addition, one of the originally selected centers was inside a correctional facility and another was located in an area heavily guarded by the military, limiting accessibility for the study. These two facilities were replaced with the support of the Department of Statistics, for a final total PHCC sample of 122 centers (table 3.1). This sample size represents approximately 55 percent of all PHCCs that have a daily utilization of at least 35 patients and about a third of all PHCCs nationally. At the request of the Ministry of Health (MOH), a sample of comprehensive health centers (CHCCs) (n=35) was also chosen, but given differences in size, staffing, and service lines, they are not included in the present analyses.

Respondent Selection
Within each PHCC, the CMO and all health providers in pediatrics, family medicine, and general medicine were selected for participation in the study. Among facilities that had a local health committee, a committee representative was invited to participate. The committee chair was the preferred choice, but if s/he was unavailable on the day of data collection, or if the CMO served as the head of the committee, then another committee member was invited to participate. Patients were selected for the study if they had received care on the day of the study visit from a clinician practicing internal medicine, pediatrics, family medicine, or general medicine. Respondents were 18 years of age or older, but

Table 3.1 Number of Primary Health Facilities Sampled by Governorate

Governorate	Number of primary health care centers
Amman	33
Ajloun	4
Aqaba	3
Balqa	9
Irbid	32
Jerash	5
Karak	5
Ma'an	3
Madaba	3
Mafraq	8
Tafileh	1
Zarqa	16
Total	**122**

eligible patients could be of any age. Patients reported on their own care, except for minors or individuals with cognitive impairment. In these cases, the most knowledgeable adult aged 18 years or older was the respondent. If more than one member of a household received services on the day of the visit, the patient whose birthday was closest to the visit date was chosen, unless both an adult and a child received services. In that case, the adult was chosen for participation. Patients were ineligible for participation if there was no adult aged 18 years or older to respond, if the respondent was attending the clinic for nonclinical purposes (for example, administrative issues only, or to visit a staff member for personal reasons), or if the patient received services outside of the clinical targets. Patients who were visibly crying or moaning were not approached and those who reported that answering questions was overly burdensome given their poor health were not interviewed. The Director of the Directorate of Health was interviewed.

Instruments and Measures
Study instruments were developed through an iterative, consultative process, including study team members and the Governance and Service Delivery Technical Advisory Committee (TAC), which comprises stakeholders in Jordan representing the health and education sectors. Through this process, a set of instruments was developed including: a patient exit interview guide; questionnaires for the center director, center health staff, and CHC representative; and a telephone interview guide used with the Head of the Directorate of Health. Table 3.2 summarizes the content of each instrument/data source.

Given that provider effort is a complex, multifaceted construct, a multicomponent approach to measurement was taken. Drawing on prior research and measurement tools (Das, Hammer, and Leonard 2008; Das and Sohnesen 2007;

Table 3.2 Contents of Data Collection Instruments

	Patient	Directorate of health representative	Chief medical officer	Center health providers	Health committee representative
Socio-demographics	X	X	X	X	X
Health encounter details	X				
Provider effort	X				
Administrative information about the health center			X		
Directorate-level monitoring and incentives		X	X		
Center-level monitoring and incentives			X	X	
Community-level monitoring and incentives			X		X

Leonard 2008), this study operationalized effort as: (1) percent of health facility doctors and nurses absent the day of the visit, assessed through a review of clinic administrative records; (2) time spent with the patient; (3) the provision of rights-based care; and (4) clinical effort using a modified retrospective consultation review (Brock, Lange, and Leonard 2014; Leonard and Masatu 2006) with patients exiting the center the day of the study visit. Table 3.3 displays each component of this construct, specific items used to measure the construct, and its form for analysis.

The study's primary independent variable was the CMO's use of accountability mechanisms (Brinkeroff 2003) including performance monitoring, sanctions, and affiliated positive incentives. Indicators of these measures were broadly based on the service provision literature (Health Systems 20/20 2012; World Health Organization 2010a) with an emphasis on personnel management practices. Measurement of these activities was accomplished through surveys of health providers at each facility, and included an assessment of the degree of monitoring providers were subject to, as well as specific types of positive incentives and sanctions used by CMOs to hold providers accountable. The extent of monitoring was modeled as a latent factor of the frequency with which the CMO: monitors provider attendance (never [0] to daily [4]); joins healthcare providers for their clinics (never [0] to weekly or more frequently [7]); and holds staff and/or bilateral meetings (never [0] to daily [6]). Sanctions were assessed by asking providers if there were consequences (that is, interrogation, verbal warning, written warning, report, deduction in payment) in their center for unexcused absences, tardiness, performing below expectations, and recurrent early departure from their assigned shift. Since less than 10 percent of providers indicated the presence of financial sanctions, financial versus nonfinancial sanctions could not be separated for analyses. Therefore, the variable was modeled as binary, meaning that sanctions were either present or absent at their facility for the behavior. A sum across the behaviors was created to create

Table 3.3 Measures of Provider Effort

Provider effort dimension	Instrument	Item(s)/instrument question	Measurement
Provider absenteeism	CMO Survey	• Review of clinic administrative records to ascertain percent of doctors and nurses assigned to the center who were not present the day of data collection.	Percent absent at center i.[a]
Time with provider	Patient exit interview	• How much time did you spend with a provider?	Average response of patients (sum of time with doctor and nurse/midwife) at center i.
Rights-based practice	Patient exit interview	• Did a healthcare provider explain your/the patient's treatment plan? • Were you involved in the decision making of the treatment plan? • The provider explained things in a way that was easy to understand? • I/the patient could talk privately to the provider? • My/the patient's treatments/exams were conducted in private? • I/the patient was treated with respect? • I/the patient had time to ask questions?	Average number of "True" answers at center i.

Compliance with CPGs	Patient exit interview	• Did a healthcare provider:
		  – take notes while you/the patient was/were speaking;
		  – listen to your/the patient's description of the illness (or reason for the visit);
		  – ask you/the patient if there were other symptoms different from the main complaint (or reason for the visit);
		  – take your/the patient's temperature;
		  – take your/patient's pulse;
		  – check your/the patient's blood pressure;
		  – measure your/the patient's height/length and weight;
		  – conduct a bed examination for you/the patient?
			Average number of "Yes" answers at center i.

a. All survey instruments were piloted prior to the main study and translated.
Note: CMO = chief medical officer.

a sanctions score (range 0–4). Since most respondents reported a high degree of sanctions, a binary variable was created to represent either greater (score greater than 3) or lesser (score of 3 or less) use of sanctions. The presence of financial rewards and recognition was also assessed for consistent attendance, timeliness, attendance during the entire shift, and performing up to or above expectations. Less than 1 percent of providers reported the presence of financial rewards, making it unsuitable for modeling and leaving only nonfinancial rewards for analysis. A sum across the distinct behaviors was created to construct a rewards score (range 0–4). Similar to the sanctions measure, nonfinancial rewards were rarely offered. Therefore, a binary measure was created to represent either greater (score greater than 2) or lesser (score of 2 or less) use of nonfinancial rewards based on the distribution of the variable. Table 3.4 displays each measure of within-facility accountability, constituent items, and its form for analysis.

Table 3.4 Measures of Within-Facility Accountability

Accountability dimension	Instrument	Item(s)/instrument question	Measurement
Monitoring	Health Provider Survey	• How often does the CMO monitor your attendance? • How frequently does the CMO join you for your clinic? • How frequently does this center have staff meetings or the CMO holds bilateral meetings with you?	Factor analysis, a method by which separate items measuring one underlying concept are summarized into a score, using the average response to each item at center *i*.

Sanctions	Health Provider Survey	• Are there any repercussions (sanction by CMO) at your center for:
		  – unexcused absences;
		  – recurrent tardiness;
		  – recurrent early departure from assigned shift; and
		  – performing below expectations?
			Average number of "yes" responses among providers at center *i* dichotomized at greater than a score of 3.

Nonfinancial rewards	Health Provider Survey	• Are there rewards (recognition by the CMO) at your center for:
		  – consistent attendance;
		  – consistent timeliness;
		  – consistent performance of entire assigned shift; and
		  – performing to or above expectations?
			Average number of "yes" responses among providers at center *i*, dichotomized at greater than a score of 2.

Financial rewards	Health Provider Survey	• Are there rewards (financial reward by the CMO) at your center for:
		  – consistent attendance;
		  – consistent timeliness;
		  – consistent performance of entire assigned shift; and
		  – performing to or above expectations?
			Frequency of "yes" responses tabulated individually because of infrequent use. Measure not used in regression analysis.

Note: CMO = chief medical officer.

Finally, several factors (delineated in table 3.5) were considered potential alternative explanations (confounders) at the patient, provider, CMO, and facility levels of the relationship between within-facility monitoring/incentives and provider effort.

Directorate- and community-level monitoring, positive incentives, and sanctions were assessed through the health provider and CMO surveys to understand the degree to which representatives from these two levels directly monitor, incentivize, and sanction staff behavior. The extent of top-down monitoring was modeled as the average frequency (from never [0] to weekly or more frequently [7]) with which a representative from the Directorate of Health/ MOH/ RMS joins the healthcare providers for their clinics. Top-down sanctions were assessed by asking providers if there were consequences (that is, interrogation, verbal warning, written warning, report, deduction in payment) meted out in their center by the Directorate, MOH, or RMS for unexcused absences, tardiness, performing below expectations, and recurrent early departure from their assigned shift. Response options were treated as binary—top-down sanctions

Table 3.5 Potential Confounding Factors

Construct	Instrument	Item(s)/instrument question	Measurement
Top-down monitoring	Health Provider Survey	• How often does a supervisor/ representative from the Directorate of Health/RMS join you for your clinic?	Average response among providers at center i.
Top-down sanctions	Health Provider Survey	• Are there any repercussions (sanction by Directorate of Health/MOH/RMS) at your center for: – unexcused absences; – recurrent tardiness; – recurrent early departure from assigned shift; or – performing below expectations?	Average number of "yes" responses among providers at center i.
Top-down nonfinancial rewards	Health Provider Survey	• Are there rewards (recognition by Directorate of Health/MOH/RMS) at your center for: – consistent attendance; – consistent timeliness; – consistent performance of entire assigned shift; or – performing to or above expectations?	Frequency of "yes" responses tabulated individually because of overall infrequent use. Measure not used in regression analysis.
Top-down financial rewards	Health Provider Survey	• Are there rewards (financial reward by Directorate of Health/MOH/RMS) at your center for: – consistent attendance; – consistent timeliness; – consistent performance of entire assigned shift; or – performing to or above expectations?	Frequency of "yes" responses tabulated individually because of infrequent use. Measure not used in regression analysis.
Bottom-up monitoring	CMO Survey	• Is there a Community Health Committee at this center?	Response by CMO at center i.
Self-rated health	Patient exit interview	• Overall, would you say that the patient's/ your health is (poor [1] to excellent [5])?	Average response among patients at center i.
Socioeconomic status	Patient exit interview	• What was your total household annual income before taxes last year (<50 [1] JD to 700 JD or more [9])?	Average response among patients at center i.
Percent of care provided that is preventive	Patient exit interview	• What is the reason you/the patient visited the center today (routine visit or medical problem/concern)? • Select type of routine visit (check-up, types of maternal and child health services, follow-up for chronic condition). *Measure combined responses from both items to generate an indicator for whether visit was for preventive care or not.*	Average response among patients at facility i leading to a percent of care received that was preventive in nature.
Receipt of continuing medical education	Provider Survey	• In the past three years, have you received any form of continuous medical/health training?	Average response among providers at center i.
Receipt of postgraduate medical training	CMO Survey	• Did you do any post-graduate training or fellowship?	Response by CMO at center i.
Facility accreditation	CMO Survey	• Has this center been accredited by the Health Care Accreditation Council (no/not yet, once, more than once)?	Response by CMO at center i.

Note: CMO = chief medical officer; MOH = Ministry of Health; RMS = Royal Medical Service.

were either present or absent at their facility for the behavior. A sum across the behaviors was created to create a sanctions score (range 0–4). The presence of top-down financial rewards and recognition was also assessed for consistent attendance, timeliness, attendance during the entire shift, and performing up to or above expectations. Similar to within-facility rewards, top-down financial rewards were almost nonexistent (less than 1 percent of health providers reported any top-down financial rewards) and nonfinancial rewards were only somewhat more frequently reported (8 percent of health providers reported any top-down nonfinancial reward). Therefore, only top-down sanctions could be modeled analytically. Bottom-up monitoring was assessed as whether or not the clinic had a CHC.

To provide a more in-depth examination of provider effort and accountability, many of the items listed in the tables above were presented to more than one respondent (for example, the health provider and the CMO), using similar wording where possible. Where relevant, these additional items are described in the results section.

Administration of the Instruments
At each facility, enumerators administered the questionnaires to the CMO, health providers, and local health committee representative using a tablet computer. While this process was underway, another enumerator conducted the patient exit interviews with patients who had received services from the pediatric, family medicine, and general medicine clinics of the health facility.

Statistical Analyses
Summary statistics were generated to examine the distribution of the various measures of provider effort and the use of sanctions. In addition, the relationship among the provider effort variables was examined with a correlation matrix to understand how strongly the variables related to one another and to ensure that they were not so highly correlated as to be substitutes for one another. In addition, the relationship between within-facility accountability measures and accountability originating from the Directorate and the community was examined with a correlation matrix. To examine the relationship between accountability and provider effort, multilevel linear regression models were constructed for each of the four measures of provider effort (absenteeism, compliance with CPGs, provision of rights-based care, and time with provider). For each outcome, an interaction between within-facility monitoring and sanctions was tested to determine if the relationship between monitoring and provider effort was different in clinics in which sanctions were used to a greater extent compared to those in which sanctions were less frequently used. Tests for an interaction between monitoring and rewards were originally intended. However, the extremely skewed distribution of the nonfinancial incentives (that is, the vast majority of clinics did not have a positive incentive environment) precluded such a test. Additional statistical detail is provided in appendix C.

Results

Study results are subsequently provided, starting with descriptive findings of the measures of provider effort and accountability, followed by results of the regression analyses. These data stem from interviews with 2,101 patients and surveys of 772 healthcare providers, 122 CMOs, and 50 CHC representatives.

Patient, Provider, and Clinic Characteristics

Among the patients attending the clinics, patients reported earning between JD 300–399 per year on average. Approximately 15 percent of patients surveyed were attending the clinic for preventive care as opposed to curative care, and average patient health was reported to be very good. Among the providers, over half reported receiving continuing medical education in the prior three years and three-quarters of CMOs reported postgraduate training. Thirty percent of the centers were accredited.

Variability in Provider Effort

Provider effort was variable. Average absenteeism in the PHCCs was 17 percent (MOH records indicate that most absences were excused). Patients reported spending approximately 10 minutes with a provider (doctor and/or nurse), ranging from 4–24 minutes. On average, clinicians performed about half of the eight methods of clinical assessment, with note taking and verbal assessments conducted much more frequently than measurement of vital signs (table 3.6). A bed examination was performed in about half of the encounters on average.

According to patient reports, healthcare providers delivered rights-based care, scoring an average of six out of seven behaviors assessed. Table 3.7 describes the frequency of each of the items inquired about. The only item not overwhelmingly positively reported by patients was patient involvement in treatment plan decisions. Only about half of the patients reported participating in treatment decisions.

Overall, the various measures of provider effort were related to one another (table 3.8). Clinics in which a higher percentage of healthcare providers were absent were also more likely to have providers who on average exerted less effort

Table 3.6 Percentage of Healthcare Providers Following CPGs (N = 2,101)

Clinical Practice Guidelines	Yes	No	Refuse to answer/ don't know/NA
Take notes	68.92	29.41	1.67
Listen to the description of the illness	82.91	7.09	10.00
Ask about other symptoms	85.25	14.75	0.00
Take temperature	23.08	75.44	0.76
Take pulse	16.71	82.39	0.90
Check blood pressure	21.94	77.49	0.57
Measure height/length and weight	12.95	86.44	0.62
Conduct a bed examination	49.45	50.45	0.10

Table 3.7 Percentage of Providers Practicing Rights-Based Care (N = 2,101)

Measures for Rights-Based Care	Yes	No	Refuse to answer/ don't know/NA
Provider explained the treatment plan[a]	84.36	15.06	0.58
Patient involved in deciding the treatment plan[a]	47.39	52.24	0.37
Provider explained things in a way that was easy to understand	86.39	8.23	5.38
Patient could talk privately to the provider	89.67	7.66	2.67
Exam was conducted in private	82.91	7.09	10.00
Patient was treated with respect	96.19	2.09	1.71
Patient had time to ask questions	86.96	5.95	7.09

a. N = 1,899 because 202 did not receive a treatment during the encounter.

Table 3.8 Correlations between Indicators of Provider Effort (N = 122)

	Absenteeism	Clinical practice guidelines	Rights-based care	Time with provider
Absenteeism	1.00			
Clinical practice guidelines	−0.20*	1.00		
Rights-based care	−0.15	0.40**	1.00	
Time with provider	−0.12	0.53**	0.24**	1.00

Note: Numbers represent correlation coefficients.
*$p < .05$; **$p < .01$.

in the clinical encounter; and there was a trend, although not statistically significant, for lower provision of rights-based care and shorter clinical encounters in clinics in which absenteeism was higher. As expected, positive relationships were detected between greater time in the clinical encounter and greater clinical effort and the provision of rights-based care.

The correlations were not so high as to suggest that one form of provider effort was a substitute for another. Therefore, all measures of provider effort were retained to generate a more comprehensive assessment compared to that gained using any one indicator alone.

Within-Facility Accountability Mechanisms in PHCCs Characterized by High Level of Monitoring, Limited Nonfinancial Rewards, Nonexistent Financial Rewards, and Uniformity in Sanctions

By design, the monitoring score had a mean of 0 and a SD of 1. Among the score's components, according to the health providers, staff meetings were held monthly, the CMOs joined them for their clinics approximately twice weekly, and attendance was monitored daily. Nearly all CMOs (97 percent) reported tracking attendance. Most providers reported the presence of sanctions in their clinics for absenteeism (84 percent), tardiness (85 percent), and early departure from their shift (79 percent). A minority of healthcare providers reported recognition for regular attendance (30 percent), consistently arriving on time (29 percent), and consistently performing their entire shift (30 percent). Less than 1 percent of healthcare providers reported financial incentives for these same behaviors, but this is not surprising given that financing of public PHCCs is carried out centrally, with limited financial autonomy of CMOs over facility budgets. Overall, absenteeism is a regularly monitored, clearly sanctioned, and poorly positively incentivized behavior in the PHCC environment.

Almost all (95 percent) CMOs reported conducting observations or carrying out clinical record audits at least monthly. When asked specifically about actions taken to ensure adherence to CPGs, 70 percent of CMOs reported that they personally observe their providers' clinics, 45 percent reported conducting patient clinical audits, and 41 percent reported training their providers as a mechanism to ensure adherence. Fourteen percent, however, reported doing nothing to ensure adherence to CPGs. Adherence to CPGs was hampered in some clinics (22 percent) by a total lack of CPG use and 17 percent of centers had not been provided with guidelines, according to CMOs. Nearly 30 percent of healthcare providers reported that guidelines pertaining to their area of responsibility had not been provided to the clinic. Therefore, while a high degree of monitoring is reported by CMOs and healthcare providers, monitoring that is intentionally geared toward guideline adherence occurs less often and the lack of guideline provision and use in some clinics effectively undermines adherence.

Overall, most healthcare providers (65 percent) reported the presence of sanctions for performing below expectations; similar to the findings for attendance, less than a third (32 percent) reported the presence of recognition for performing beyond expectations. Financial incentives for performing well were rare (reported by less than 1 percent of healthcare providers), but again not surprising in light of the limited financial autonomy at the facility level referred to previously. On balance, the average PHCC environment was one in which within-facility monitoring was present, nonfinancial rewards were infrequent, financial rewards were nearly nonexistent, and sanctions were almost uniformly in place.

Top-Down and Bottom-Up Accountability Mechanisms Are Linked to Within-Facility Monitoring and Sanctions Practice

The frequency of top-down monitoring and sanctions was somewhat similar to within-facility monitoring and sanctions practice as can be seen by the significant positive correlations between within-facility and top-down accountability monitoring and sanctions presented in table 3.9 and by health provider reports. According to health providers, representatives from the Directorate, MOH, or RMS joined them for their clinics quarterly, on average. This ranged from a frequency of not even once a year to at least weekly. Similar to the within-facility findings, nearly all behaviors investigated were sanctioned, although with differing frequency. Absenteeism was the most consistently reported sanctioned behavior, with 76 percent of health providers reporting the presence of this sanction. Recurrent tardiness (73 percent) and recurrent early departure from the shift were nearly as often mentioned sanctions (69 percent). Performing below expectations was mentioned by just over half of the providers (53 percent). Top-down

Table 3.9 Correlations between Within-Facility and Top-Down and Bottom-Up Measures of Accountability (N = 122)

	Within facility monitoring	Within facility sanctions	Within facility nonfinancial rewards
Top-down monitoring	0.358**	0.235**	0.029
Top-down sanctions	0.207*	0.768**	0.143
Bottom-up monitoring	0.055	0.060	0.289**

Note: Numbers represent correlation coefficients.
*$p < .05$; **$p < .01$.

monitoring and sanctions were not associated with CMOs' use of nonfinancial rewards, although bottom-up monitoring was (table 3.9), suggesting some role for CHCs in supporting the CMO's use of rewards for quality enhancing behavior. Only 43 percent of clinics had a CHC, suggesting that many communities lack formal bottom-up mechanisms to monitor clinic performance. According to the CHC representatives surveyed, committees, where present, monitored overall clinic performance on average twice a year, suggesting at least a moderate level of bottom-up monitoring among clinics with a CHC. CHCs varied in their monitoring function, with some not monitoring clinic performance at all and others reporting that they monitor clinic performance monthly. Much greater information on what the monitoring entailed is needed to better capitalize on the potential benefits of this accountability mechanism.

CMO Monitoring Highly Correlated with High Provider Effort, But Not with Absenteeism

Results from the multilevel regression models are presented in table C.1 and subsequently described.

Each within-facility accountability mechanism (monitoring, sanctions, and rewards) was examined for its independent relationship to provider effort. Among the accountability mechanisms examined, monitoring proved to be the most consistent correlate of higher provider effort. In clinics in which the CMO monitored health providers more closely, health providers exerted greater clinical effort ($p < .01$), provided more rights-based and responsive care ($p < .05$), and spent more time with patients in clinical examinations ($p < .05$). Monitoring was not independently related to absenteeism, potentially because absenteeism is already so frequently monitored in centers and sanctioned by the CMO and Directorate. CMO sanctions, when considered independently, either were not associated with provider effort (absenteeism, time spent with the provider) or were associated with poorer effort and rights-based practice, such that health providers exerted less clinical effort during exams and were less respectful of patients' rights when providing care. This may suggest that a high sanctions environment is present in clinics in which provider effort is poor, or that sanctions are not producing the desired outcome. This cannot be discerned from the cross-sectional data. CMOs' use of nonfinancial rewards to recognize good behavior and excellent clinical practice was not associated with provider effort.

However, this form of incentive was very infrequently used, limiting this study's ability to assess its effectiveness as a tool for enhancing accountability.

Monitoring Associated with Greater Provision of Rights-Based Care in High Sanctions Environment

In addition to the main effects of accountability mechanisms, this study tested whether the impact of monitoring on provider effort was different depending on the degree to which sanctions were also used to hold providers accountable. This effect was tested for each type of provider effort, but found to be significant only for the provision of rights-based care (figure 3.5). In an environment of low sanctions, monitoring has little impact on the provision of care, and because rights-based care was provided at a high level at most facilities, perhaps because of the lack of monitoring specifically on this aspect of care. Alternatively, in environments where sanctions are present for nearly every behavior assessed, monitoring is associated with greater provision of rights-based care.

Among the top-down and bottom-up accountability mechanisms, a few stand out, specifically top-down sanctions, which are associated with providers spending more time with patients and lower provider absenteeism. As noted above, absenteeism and other behaviors related to provider presence in the clinic such as recurrent tardiness and recurrent early departure from shift were recognized by most health providers to be sanctionable offenses. The cross-sectional nature of the data makes it difficult to know if the presence of sanctions serves to deter effort lapses or to punish them, or both. However, directorate-level supervision carries additional weight and power since the decision to terminate a staff member is made at the directorate/MOH level, not at the facility level. Therefore, sanctions may be used punitively within the facility, but may serve as a deterrent when issued by the more powerful directorate. This explanation, while plausible,

Figure 3.5 Relationship between Monitoring and Rights-Based Care, by Sanction Level (90% CI)

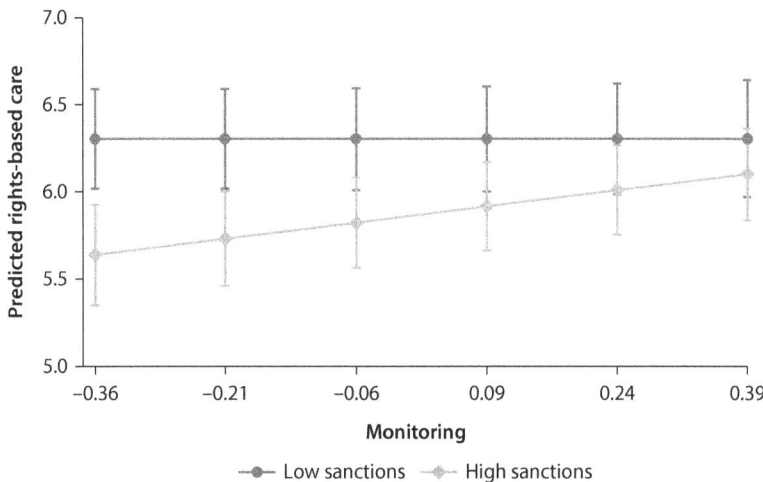

does not explain the inverse association between top-down monitoring and both rights-based care and time with the provider. Monitoring may function differently when performed by the CMO compared to a representative from the directorate. However, the study cannot discern potential differences. Bottom-up monitoring through a CHC was associated with greater provision of rights-based care. Similarly, in accredited facilities, providers spent more time on average with patients than in centers that were not accredited.

Notably, neither the health provider's report of training in the prior three years nor the CMO's receipt of postgraduate training was related to the various measures of provider effort. In fact, having received postgraduate training was associated with less time spent per patient. While more detailed information is needed to understand potential links between different types of training and provider effort, as some differences may be obscured by considering all types of training together, the finding does suggest that training alone is not sufficient to enhance effort as measured by this study.

Study Limitations

More research is needed to examine some of the inconsistencies found across types of provider effort and level of accountability, preferably using a mixture of data collection formats since the present study relied almost entirely on self-reporting. The study attempted to avoid bias from the provision of socially desirable responses through the review of clinic administrative records for attendance and the analysis of data provided by health providers, patients, and CHC representatives in the regression analyses. To minimize the influence of employees or patients who might have a vested interest in responding overly positively or negatively, responses were sought from all health providers in a facility and 25 patients per facility, and responses were averaged at the facility level for the primary analyses. Questionnaire items were worded to elicit as objective a response as possible, avoiding language to suggest the presence of a "correct" response. Still, socially desirable responses cannot be ruled out. Furthermore, given the asymmetry of information about the quality of care received, and the inclusion of patients receiving a variety of preventive and curative care, only a narrow range of key clinical procedures could be assessed through patient reports. While it is beneficial to assess patients' experiences across the major primary care service lines, the breadth of clinical experiences limited the range of clinical procedures that could be assessed to those that are likely present across preventative and curative, adult and pediatric care. In addition, more service line or disease-specific research is needed to ascertain whether accurate and appropriate care was provided. Future work should examine these relationships over time to enable an assessment of cause and effect, which is confounded in the present study by its cross-sectional design. While this study includes a nationally representative sample of PHCCs, its findings pertain only to those with daily patient loads of at least 35 patients and potential differences between urban and rural facilities cannot be investigated. Finally, complex analyses were performed on a relatively small sample size, which limits the study's power to detect relationships.

The Last Mile to Quality Service Delivery in Jordan • http://dx.doi.org/10.1596/978-1-4648-1069-5

Conclusions

Overall, the findings from this study characterize the degree and type of accountability mechanisms operating in Jordan's PHCCs and their relationship to provider effort, with an emphasis on within-facility accountability. Results show that within-facility monitoring seems to improve provider effort. Bottom-up monitoring is potentially also beneficial, especially to encourage rights-based clinical care, but more research is needed in this area. Sanctions at the facility level likely serve more of a disciplinary function rather than acting as a deterrent when considered independently of other accountability practices. However, within-facility use of sanctions does seem to enhance the impact of monitoring on the provision of rights-based practice. From another perspective, accreditation seems to support longer clinical encounters and as shown in prior research, accreditation is associated with improved health outcomes in Jordanian hospitals (Halasa and others 2015). This strategy is currently underutilized as a minority of clinics are accredited. The accreditation process involves a range of quality-enhancing changes, including the establishment of a CHC. While it is challenging for citizens who are not medically trained to monitor provider effort in the same manner as a CMO, the committee can serve as a channel for community preferences and grievances and can leverage its power to incentivize greater provider effort.

Notes

1. This is not to say that the knowledge of medical providers is not an important determinant of patient outcomes. Studies have found a serious lack of knowledge among healthcare providers in developing countries, and this lack of knowledge is often disastrous for patients. Furthermore, in their comprehensive review of healthcare in low-income countries, Das and Hammer (2014) find that all the studies they examined found a strong correlation between education and knowledge.

2. Unfortunately, there are no empirical studies of this from the MENA region. In fact, this is one of the biggest contributions of the current study. However, it is important to note that given that these are studies on behavior of providers they should be transferable across settings at least to some degree.

3. Chief medical officers (CMOs) are referred to as Heads of Healthcare Center (HOHCs) in Jordan. This report uses the conventional terminology of CMO to be consistent with existing literature.

References

Abu-Kharmeh, S. Suleiman. 2012. "Evaluating the Quality of Health Care Services in the Hashemite Kingdom of Jordan." *International Journal of Business and Management* 7 (4): 195–205.

Al-Qutob, Raeda, and Laeth S. Nasir. 2008. "Provider Perceptions of Reproductive Health Service Quality in Jordanian Public Community Health Centers." *Health Care Women International* 29 (5): 539–50.

Banerjee, Abhijit, Angus Deaton, and Esther Duflo. 2004. "Health, Health Care, and Economic Development: Wealth, Health, and Health Services in Rural Rajasthan." *American Economic Review* 94 (2): 326–30.

Banerjee, Abhijit, and Esther Duflo. 2006. "Addressing Absence." *Journal of Economic Perspectives* 20 (1): 117–32.

Banerjee, Abhijit V., Rachel Glennerster, and Esther Duflo. 2008. "Putting a Band-Aid on a Corpse: Incentives for Nurses in the Indian Public Health Care System." *Journal of the European Economic Association* 6: 487–500.

Björkman, Martina, and Jakob Svensson. 2010. "When Is Community-Based Monitoring Effective? Evidence from a Randomized Experiment in Primary Health in Uganda." *Journal of the European Economic Association* 8 (2–3): 571–81.

Brinkeroff, Derick. 2003. "Accountability and Health Systems: Overview, Framework, and Strategies." Partners for Health Reformplus Abt Associates Inc., Bethesda, MD.

Brock, J. Michelle, Andreas Lange, and Kenneth L. Leonard. 2014. "Giving and Promising Gifts: Experimental Evidence on Reciprocity from the Field." Working Paper 165, European Bank for Reconstruction and Development, London.

Callen, Michael Joseph, Saad Gulzar, Syed Ali Hasanain, and Muhammad Yasir Khan. 2013. "The Political Economy of Public Employee Absence: Experimental Evidence from Pakistan." SSRN Working Paper 2316245, Social Science Research Network, Rochester, NY. https://papers.ssrn.com/sol3/papers2.cfm?abstract_id=2316245.

Chaudhury, Nazmul, Jeffrey Hammer, Michael Kremer, Karthik Muralidharan, and F. Halsey Rogers. 2006. "Missing in Action: Teacher and Health Worker Absence in Developing Countries." *Journal of Economic Perspectives* 20 (1): 91–116.

Das, Jishnu, and Jeffrey Hammer. 2007. "Money for Nothing: The Dire Straits of Medical Practice in Delhi, India." *Journal of Development Economics* 83 (1): 1–36.

Das, Jishnu, and Paul J. Gertler. 2007. "Variations in Practice Quality in Five Low-Income Countries: A Conceptual Overview." *Health Affairs* 26 (3): w296–309.

———. 2014. "Quality of Primary Care in Low-Income Countries: Facts and Economics." *Annual Review Economics* 6 (1): 525–53.

———, and Kenneth Leonard. 2008. "The Quality of Medical Advice in Low-Income Countries." *Journal of Economic Perspectives* 22 (2): 93–114.

Das, Jishnu, Alaka Holla, Aakash Mohpal, and Karthik Muralidharan. 2013. "Quality and Accountability in Healthcare Delivery: Evidence from an Audit Study of Healthcare Providers in India." Unpublished manuscript, World Bank, Washington, DC.

Das, Jishnu, and Carolina Sánchez-Páramo. 2004. "Short but Not Sweet: New Evidence on Short Duration Morbidities from India." Working Paper, Development Research Group, World Bank, Washington, DC.

Das, J., and Thomas Pave Sohnesen. 2007. "Variations in Doctor Effort: Evidence from Paraguay." *Health Affairs (Millwood)* 26: w324–37.

Demaio, Alessandro R., Karoline Kragelund Nielsen, Britt Pinkowski Tersbol, Per Kallestrup, and Dan W. Meyrowitsch. 2014. "Primary Health Care: A Strategic Framework for the Prevention and Control of Chronic Non-communicable Disease." *Global Health Action* 7: 24504.

Ferrinho, Paulo, Wim Van Lerberghe, Inês Fronteira, Fátima Hipólito, and André Biscaia. 2004. "Dual Practice in the Health Sector: Review of the Evidence." *Human Resources for Health* 2 (1): 14.

Gertler, Paul, and Christel Vermeersch. 2012. "Using Performance Incentives to Improve Health Outcomes." Policy Research Working Paper 6100, World Bank, Washington, DC.

Halasa, Yara, Wu Zeng, Edward Chappy, and D. S. Shepard. 2015. "Value and Impact of International Hospital Accreditation: A Case Study from Jordan." *Eastern Mediterranean Health Journal* 21: 90–99.

Health Systems 20/20. 2012. "The Health System Assessment Approach: A How-To Manual." Version 2.0. http://www.healthsystemassessment.org.

Health Care Accreditation Council. 2011. Primary Health Care and Family Planning Centers Accreditation Standards (2nd ed.). Amman, Jordan: Health Care Accreditation Council.

High Health Council. 2013. *Jordan National Health Accounts 2010–2011 Technical Report 4 2013*. Amman, Jordan: High Health Council.

IHME (Institute for Health Metrics and Evaluation). 2010. "Global Burden of Disease Study (2010) Dataset." IHME, Seattle, WA.

Khatatbeh, Moawiah. 2013. "Factors Associated with High Turnover of Jordanian Physicians in Rural Areas: A Sequential Exploratory Mixed Method Study." PhD, Centre for International Health, Curtin University, Irbid. http://espace.library.curtin.edu.au/R?func=dbin.

Khoury, S. A., and S. Mawajdeh. 2004. "Performance of Health Providers in Primary Health Care Services in Jordan." *Eastern Mediterranean Health Journal* 10 (3): 372–81.

Leonard, Kenneth. 2008. "Is Patient Satisfaction Sensitive to Changes in the Quality of Care? An Exploration of the Hawthorne Effect." *Journal of Health Economics* 27: 444–59.

Leonard, Kenneth, and Melkiory C. Masatu. 2006. "Outpatient Process Quality Evaluation and the Hawthorne Effect." *Social Science & Medicine* 63: 2330–40.

Leonard, K. L., M. C. Masatu, and A. Vialou. 2007. "Getting Doctors to Do Their Best: The Roles of Ability and Motivation in Health Care." *Journal of Human Resources* 42: 682–700.

Marmot, Michael, and Richard Wilkinson, eds. 2005. *Social Determinants of Health*. 2nd ed. Oxford: Oxford University Press.

Otoom, S., A. Batieha, H. Hadidi, M. Hasan, and K. Al-Saudi. 2002. "Evaluation of Drug Use in Jordan Using WHO Patient Care and Health Facility Indicators." *Eastern Mediterranean Health Journal* 8: 544–49.

Rabie, Tamer Sameh, Björn Ekman, and Ece Amber Özçelik. 2014. "Towards Universal Health Coverage: A Comprehensive Review of the Health Financing System in Jordan." World Bank, Washington, DC.

World Bank. 2014. *World Development Indicators, 2014*. Washington, DC: World Bank.

World Health Organization. 2010a. "Monitoring the Building Blocks of Health Systems: A Handbook of Indicators and Their Measurement Strategies." World Health Organization, Geneva.

———. 2010b. *Package of Essential Noncommunicable (PEN) Disease Interventions for Primary Health Care in Low-Resource Setting*. Geneva: World Health Organization.

———. 2011. *NCD Country Profiles: Jordan*. Geneva: World Health Organization.

———. 2014. "Global Health Observatory Data Repository" (accessed April 2014). http://apps.who.int/gho/data/?theme=main. Geneva.

CHAPTER 4

Conclusions and Policy Recommendations

Effort Put Forth by Teachers and Healthcare Providers in Their Jobs Is Seemingly Low

Across both service sectors in this study, provider effort was low on average. Among the many standards to be followed in teachers' classroom instructional practice, teachers are expected to strive to provide continuous feedback to students, respond to students' questions in a way that is conducive to creating a respectful and emotionally supportive environment for learning, design a range of student assessment methods that provide a variety of performance opportunities for students, and consider specific student performance and needs while designing lessons. Yet, an analysis of data collected by the United States Agency for International Development (USAID) through classroom observations, teacher questionnaires, and student surveys of a representative sample of second and third grade classrooms in Jordan reveals that effort put forth by teachers in meeting these standards is seemingly low. Only one in five teachers mark all pages of students' copybooks, while roughly 25 percent of teachers mark only a few pages, and 3.4 percent do not mark even a single page. When a student is unable to answer a question, students report that as many as 70 percent of teachers simply repeat the exact same question to the same student again, or ask another student instead, while 5.4 percent of teachers scold the student or send her outside of the classroom or to stand in a corner. Moreover, almost two in three teachers report using only one or two methods of student assessment, and as little as one-fourth of all teachers report using these assessments to inform their lesson planning. While these findings are exclusive to teachers in early primary grades, they may be indicative of a wider challenge present across education levels in the country.[1]

Similarly, in health centers, doctors and other healthcare staff are expected to deliver appropriate care that meets technical standards while respecting patients' rights. Doctors and other staff therefore must regularly come to work on time, remain in clinic for their full shifts, abide by up-to-date clinical protocols, listen and respond to patients with respect and clarity, and spend sufficient time with patients to understand their health concerns, diagnose health conditions correctly, and prescribe appropriate treatments and, where applicable, medications. An analysis of original data collected in this study shows that provider effort is low in multiple areas. During field visits to health centers, 17 percent of health providers on average were reported absent. While some clinics operated fully staffed, others were missing over half of their providers, suggesting a lack of access to care. On the basis of interviews conducted with patients exiting healthcare facilities, study findings highlight low provider effort during the clinical encounter. On average, health providers performed only half of key exam elements, suggesting that diagnoses and other health-related decisions are being made with limited clinical information. Furthermore, these decisions occur during clinical encounters that last as little as 4 minutes. The average length of an encounter was 10 minutes, but thorough, high-quality, rights-based care is difficult to deliver in that span, let alone in 4 minutes. This was substantiated by the data. Shorter encounters were associated with lower clinical effort and lower likelihood of the provision of rights-based care, although, on average, patients reported that they received respectful, responsive, rights-based care.

Across the two sectors, significant effort gains can be made. Given the strong evidence linking provider effort to higher-quality education and healthcare, findings from these studies highlight the potential quality gains to be made through policies incentivizing greater effort in both sectors.

Increasing Principal and CMO Monitoring of Providers May Yield Tangible Improvements in Teachers' and Healthcare Providers' Effort in the Workplace

Being trained as teachers and medical doctors, having spent numerous years teaching in the classroom and providing clinical services, and sharing the same work space as the teachers and healthcare providers they oversee, school principals and chief medical officers (CMOs) are well placed to identify low levels of provider effort when they see them. Indeed, findings from this study suggest that principals and CMOs in Jordan who leverage this position of visibility by continuously monitoring teachers and healthcare providers are assisting providers to exert the effort needed to provide quality services.

In the case of education, the analyses for this study suggest that teachers put forth more effort when principals conduct classroom observations and verify their lesson plans more frequently. Teachers who were better monitored provided more feedback to students and took more steps to create a positive learning environment for students. In turn, students tend to learn better when their school principals monitor teachers more frequently, as their teachers exert higher levels of effort. This is evidenced in this study by higher math and language test scores among students whose teachers were better monitored. Findings in the health sector mimic those in education. Health providers exert greater effort in examining and treating patients and spend more time with patients when CMOs institute and carry out monitoring procedures at the facility level.

Effective Monitoring in Jordan Is a Missed Opportunity

Teachers report that only 5 percent of school principals conduct weekly class-room observations. The majority of principals (57.3 percent) observe their teach-ers' classroom instruction once every one to three months. It is alarming that 12.5 percent of principals visit classrooms only once a year, and 4.9 percent have never conducted a classroom observation according to their teachers. Principals are more likely to verify teachers' lesson plans, with 71.5 percent of them con-ducting this verification once every week. Still, roughly 8 percent of principals carry out this verification only once every one to three months, and 2 percent have never verified their teachers' lesson plans.

Health providers seem to be monitored quite frequently. According to health providers, staff meetings are held monthly, the CMOs join them for their clinics approximately once every two weeks, and attendance is monitored daily. Nearly all CMOs (97 percent) report tracking attendance and a similarly high percent (95 percent) report conducting observations or carrying out clinical record audits at least monthly. Fourteen percent, however, report doing nothing to ensure adherence to clinical practice guidelines (CPGs). While a high degree of moni-toring is reported by CMOs and healthcare providers, monitoring that is inten-tionally geared toward guideline adherence occurs less often. Given the effort-enhancing benefits of monitoring, quality gains can be made through more extensive monitoring in the education sector and better targeted monitoring in the health sector.

Reaping the Highest Values from Principal and CMO Monitoring Is Only Possible in a Strong Incentives Environment That Rewards Provider Effort More Than It Penalizes It

Despite the effort gains that are possible through appropriate monitoring, the accountability environment in Jordan's education and health sectors provides very few incentives for teachers and healthcare providers to dedicate the highest level of effort to their jobs. This relates to financial as well as nonfinancial incen-tives for providers at both the facility and the central levels.

Financial Incentives to Encourage Provider Effort Are Absent

Salary schemes for teachers and healthcare providers are only tied to providers' credentials and years of experience, providing no incentive for providers to per-form to their knowledge frontier. Furthermore, evidence from the case controlled study in education suggests a prevalent belief by teachers that they will receive an automatic promotion and salary increase after four to six years, regardless of how much effort they put forth in their jobs. The picture is no different at the facility level, where school principals and CMOs do not provide any kind of financial bonuses to incentivize high effort. On the other hand, reductions in payment are possible according to civil service regulations, although docking payment is rarely practiced. Only 19.6 percent of healthcare providers report the possibility that the Directorate of Health may dock their payment in case of absenteeism. Anecdotal evidence in education also suggests that reduction in payment is hardly used, and, when it is, it is only to penalize unjustified absenteeism.

The Accountability Environment in Jordan Leans Heavily toward Sanctions as Opposed to Recognition

Recognizing provider effort and achievements can increase motivation. Yet principals and CMOs in Jordan seldom rely on nonfinancial mechanisms to incentivize provider effort. And when they do, they mostly make use of mechanisms to sanction. Out of the six schools visited for the case controlled study in education, only one school principal was found to be systematically recognizing her teachers' level of effort by organizing "teacher of the year" contests each academic year. In the rest of schools, two-thirds of interviewed teachers expressed a very strong desire to be recognized in any way by the principal for their high effort, so as to motivate them to keep up the good work. On the other hand, teachers in a third of the schools reported the use of verbal reprimands in the presence of colleagues as a penalty for underperformance. Teachers in all visited schools agreed on the lack of any formal nonfinancial mechanism to reward or sanction teachers' effort by the Directorate of Education.

Similarly, the evidence on the health sector suggests that less than a third of all CMOs use some form of nonfinancial reward to recognize healthcare providers' effort, while roughly two-thirds use sanctions ranging from verbal admonitions to written warnings to deter providers from being absent, late, leaving early from their shift, and underperforming. In environments in which sanctions are in place for most effort-related transgressions, the impact of monitoring on provider effort is enhanced at least for some types of provider effort. In a high sanctions environment, better monitored healthcare providers are more likely to provide rights-based care than more poorly monitored providers. However, the use of sanctions was shown to be unrelated to the linkage between monitoring and other forms of provider effort, and most clinics already operate in a high sanctions environment, suggesting limited additional benefit from greater use of sanctions as an effort-enhancing strategy. The use of positive incentives, on the other hand, is a promising strategy that is currently underutilized in Jordan.

Greater Managerial Autonomy at the Facility Level Could Enhance the Relationship between Accountability and Provider Effort

In the health and education sectors, CMOs and principals have limited managerial autonomy that could support their more effective use of effort-enhancing accountability measures. In both sectors, extremely limited facility budgets preclude the use of financial incentives while the inability to hire and fire staff limits the impact of efforts to bolster provider accountability. Providing greater managerial and financial autonomy for CMOs and principals would incentive their use of accountability measures and potentially strengthen the impact of their monitoring and sanctioning efforts.

Increasing Monitoring and Strengthening the Incentives Environment Will Lead Jordan toward Performance-Based Education and Health Systems

Traditional education and health systems place seniority and education credentials at the center of their interaction with teachers and healthcare providers. These determinants inform the advancement of providers' rank in the organizational hierarchy, and the consequent impacts on salary raise. However, the imperative to improve the quality of education and health services has led many countries to instead put provider performance at the heart of this interaction. Moving toward such performance-based accountability systems requires countries to respond to four key questions, as follows.

What Indicators Will Be Used to Measure Provider Performance?

The selection of appropriate indicators to measure provider performance is of paramount importance, as this guides teachers and healthcare providers in their decision of where to allocate their effort. The adequacy of this selection rests on two main criteria. On the one hand, indicators need to have a direct impact on the broader system goals of improving quality of education and healthcare services. On the other hand, countries should select indicators that providers can directly influence. In this regard, this study presents a set of indicators that lie within providers' span of control. In other words, providers can influence these indicators by increasing their level of effort.

In the education sector, these indicators include providing continuous feedback to students, responding to students' questions in a way that is conducive to creating a respectful and emotionally supportive environment for learning, designing a range of student assessment methods that provide a variety of performance opportunities for students, and considering specific student performance and needs while designing lessons. The analysis in chapter 2 suggests that improvements in these indicators may have also directly impacted student learning in Jordan.[2]

In the health sector, indicators can track a variety of practices in facilities that can improve both the technical and the nontechnical dimensions of care. These indicators include measures of whether providers abide by clinical protocols and guidelines on the basis of clinical observation or periodic reviews of patient records; time spent with patients; provider compliance with the basic principles of rights-based care; recurrent absences, tardiness, and/or early departures from shifts by staff members; the frequency of staff meetings; and the implementation of regular performance evaluations and clear communication of professional rights and responsibilities.

How Will These Indicators Be Collected?

Given their technical expertise, their daily proximity to providers, and their implicit responsibility to continuously monitor teachers and healthcare providers, principals and CMOs should be at the frontline of data collection endeavors.

This study has identified relevant monitoring methods currently carried out by principals and CMOs in Jordan. School principals conduct classroom observations and verify teachers' lesson plans, and CMOs join providers' clinics, allowing them to directly observe different indicators of provider effort, such as the ones identified in this study.

In addition to these conventional methods, principals and CMOs should complement their monitoring efforts by gauging beneficiaries' perspectives of the quality of services they receive through student surveys and patient exit interviews. Beyond beneficiaries' satisfaction, these instruments should aim to capture what is happening at the beneficiary-provider interaction. When asked the right questions, in the right ways, students and patients can be an important source of information on what providers are doing in classrooms and clinics, contributing to cross-verify principals and CMOs' own observations (Gates Foundation 2012; Leonard 2008). The USAID student survey instrument and the developed patient exit interview instrument used under this study provide good examples of this. Administrative records should also be used when possible to complement the information received from observation and client reports. This may require changes in information systems or in how information is documented (electronically or on paper) to allow for the easy retrieval of information needed to bolster provider effort and accountability.

Yet, for these monitoring methods to meaningfully contribute toward a performance-based system, they ought to be systematized in their frequency and standardized in their documentation. As mentioned above, evidence from this study reveals that some principals conduct classroom observations every single day, while others do so only once a year. Although CMOs and health providers reported high levels of monitoring, considerably less monitoring was directed at compliance with CPGs—an essential component of safe, high-quality healthcare. Frequent observation of these indicators, through a number of different methods, is critical as it increases the likelihood of obtaining reliable indicators that produce similar results under consistent conditions. But this process should not stop here—these indicators need to be documented in a standard manner to provide a solid evidence base for providers' annual performance appraisals and communicated to the directorate level. It is important to note that the collection and documentation should occur across all facilities and audits of CMOs' and principals' use of accountability mechanisms and provider effort could be performed on a regular basis by the directorate as part of the top-down monitoring function.

Although principals and CMOs should be at the frontline of monitoring endeavors, the independent verification role of the Directorates of Education and Health is also key. Directorate inspectors should corroborate the indicators reported by principals through periodic—and to the extent possible unannounced—visits to the providers. In this regard, evidence from this study indicates that roughly 60 percent of schools receive monthly visits from directorate supervisors, while nearly 23 percent of schools are visited only once a year or not at all. In the health sector, providers reported that representatives from the directorate joined them for their clinics quarterly on average, but this was not a uniform practice, with some providers reporting almost no direct monitoring and others reporting being joined by a directorate representative at least weekly. Therefore, a considerable degree of inconsistency exists in directorate-level monitoring of provider behavior. Beyond the need for periodic visits from directorate inspectors, the use of common metrics that mirror those used by the principals are key to ensure a quality verification process.

What Actions Will Be Taken in Light of These Indicators?

With reliable indicators of provider performance in their hands, the next question to address is what principals, CMOs, and ministries will do with this information. Reward and sanction schemes need to be devised and tied to performance indicators to incentivize a change in provider effort. At the facility level, the use of nonfinancial rewards (such as recognition of good performance through "employee-of-the-month" or other types of awards and opportunities for additional training that are tied to performance) are a promising course of action in Jordan that can be implemented in the short run, at very little cost. At the central level, the need to tie promotions and salary increases of teachers and healthcare providers to performance indicators cannot be overemphasized, and is well within reach in Jordan. With the largest share of Jordan's education and health expenditures devoted to salaries, ensuring that salary increases are merit based has the potential to significantly increase efficiency in the allocation of public resources, while at the same time aligning system incentives toward the goal of improving the quality of education and healthcare.

In the medium to long term, more sophisticated pay for performance (P4P) schemes that are closely linked to quality of service delivery can be explored, tailored, and incrementally implemented in the Jordanian context, bringing Jordan to the forefront of performance-based systems along with some of the most advanced countries in the world. The design of P4P schemes should benefit from the growing body of research on the use of these schemes in both sectors, including the appropriate size of incentives, strategies for the mitigation of potential unanticipated consequences, sources of funding and resource flows, individual versus group incentives, an orientation toward positive and not punitive incentives, as well as the necessary implementation arrangements and monitoring and evaluation mechanisms around them.

How This Be Addressed through a Systems Approach?

Performance-Based Accountability Is One of the Links of Effective Performance Management Systems

Performance-based accountability is one of the key links in performance management systems (PMS), but not the only one. As such, it needs to be fully incorporated into existing PMS, creating synergies with all other elements in the system.

At the facility level, principals and CMOs ought to effectively communicate specific expectations for teaching and clinical practice to providers in light of the performance indicators against which they would be held accountable.

Moreover, their role in creating an adequate supportive environment for providers that is conducive to eliciting the highest level of effort is essential. This includes ensuring all necessary equipment and supplies are present at the facility and are well functioning. In a constrained budget environment, principals and CMOs should be very strategic in prioritizing those structural factors that are especially important for providers to achieve performance indicators.

Last, paramount to an effective PMS and a natural extension of their monitoring efforts is the technical leadership role that principals and CMOs should play in their facilities (Education First and Gates Foundation 2015). Beyond providing teachers and health providers with a summative assessment through the annual performance appraisal, the provision of actionable, formative feedback should be built into the ongoing monitoring mechanisms and incentive schemes of principals and CMOs, ensuring that providers striving to improve their efforts in the classroom and clinics are well aware of how they can do so.

Performance Indicators Are Highly Valuable for Strategic Professional Development Planning

At the central level, effective personnel management systems use two main pillars to ensure continuous improvement in provider performance. On the one hand, and as discussed above, strong performance-based accountability systems are required to incentivize the highest level of effort by providers. On the other hand, and building on this first pillar, ministries need to closely examine providers' performance indicators to refine and purposefully target teacher professional development and continuous medical education programs. Furthermore, and beyond their clear relevance to inform in-the-job training programs, performance indicators provide ministries with a wealth of information to identify specific areas of strength as well as areas for growth of teachers and healthcare providers that can inform preservice education and certification programs in Jordan.

Adequate Accountability and Training Are Required for Principals and CMOs to Champion Such an Important Undertaking

If principals and CMOs in Jordan are to become the primary champions of a strong performance-based accountability system for teachers and healthcare providers, they should be subject to an accountability system that ensures they meet their monitoring functions and their technical leadership roles to the best of their ability. The role of the Directorates of Education and Health in systematically monitoring and verifying principal and CMO practices, coupled with the provision of financial and nonfinancial incentives to motivate them, is key. Similarly important is the need to provide the necessary training—both preservice and in-service—to ensure that principals and CMOs are well equipped to champion such an important undertaking.

In sum, this study has shown that Jordan's education and health sectors can greatly benefit from instituting more effective monitoring and incentive systems to enhance provider effort for better education and health outcomes. The role of school principals and CMOs in this respect cannot be overemphasized given their knowledge and proximity to interactions that take place at the student-teacher and patient-health provider interface. The move toward a performance-based system in both sectors is a sound overall policy reform that the Government of Jordan would be advised to further pursue. This calls for reorientation of the system in a way that ensures more efficiency by linking pay to productivity and a focus on quality. Arrangements to achieve efficiency may also be seen as equitable if they fairly reward provider performance. To realize this, such systems need to uphold performance-based accountability and strongly integrate it within existing PMS.

The government of Jordan would be advised to initially pilot the recommended course of action presented in this report on a small scale, which can then be rolled-out contingent on positive outcomes measured through impact evaluations. The design of such a pilot program and its idiosyncrasies would be informed by consultations with stakeholders in both sectors in Jordan. As previously described, the pilot would need to carefully consider a number of key design features, including inter alia: criteria to measure performance; specificities related to performance appraisal systems; feedback mechanisms; the right mix of extrinsic, as well as intrinsic, rewards and sanctions; appropriate quantum of pay subject to performance criteria; evaluation schemes; implementation arrangements; and overall governance mechanisms.

Although Jordan's overall education and health systems have fared well over the past two decades, the recommendations presented in this report based on findings from the two sectoral studies provide an even stronger impetus to push Jordan to the forefront in both sectors. It is high time that Jordan reaps the benefits of its investments in health and education. The focus on provider effort and quality under an effective accountability system is at the heart of reform and cannot be stressed enough.

Notes

1. The Classroom Observation Phase II Study, prepared in 2015 by the National Center for Human Resources Development in Jordan, documents a positive trend in teacher practices in the country in the 2011–14 period. Specifically, using classroom observations, the study reports improvements in classroom management, student-centered teaching, and student assessment, as measured by a standardized classroom observation tool. These positive trends are certainly encouraging. Yet, as elaborated in the present study, more is required to bring teachers' efforts (or practices) up to their knowledge frontier.

2. Careful consideration of these four areas is fundamental as the country develops teacher performance assessments based on the National Teacher Professional Standards under the Second Education Reform for the Knowledge Economy (ERfKE II). It is also highly informative in the Ministry of Education's ongoing endeavor in establishing an accountability and quality assurance mechanism to incentivize stakeholders in the education system to improve learning in Jordan's public schools.

References

Education First and Gates Foundation. 2015. "Giving Teachers the Feedback and Support They Deserve: Five Essential Practices." Education First and Gates Foundation, Seattle, WA.

Gates Foundation. 2012. "Gathering Feedback for Teaching: Combining High-Quality Observations with Student Surveys and Achievement Gains." MET Project Research Paper, Seattle, WA.

Leonard, K. L. 2008. "Is Patient Satisfaction Sensitive to Changes in the Quality of Care? An Exploration of the Hawthorne Effect." *Journal of Health Economics* 27: 444–59.

Education Sector

Table A.1 Framework for Teaching

Domain 1: Planning and preparation

  1a Demonstrating knowledge of content and pedagogy

  1b Demonstrating knowledge of students

  1c Setting instructional outcomes

  1d Demonstrating knowledge of resources

  1e Designing coherent instruction

  1f Designing student assessments

Domain 2: Classroom environment

  2a Creating an environment of respect and rapport

  2b Establishing a culture for learning

  2c Managing classroom procedures

  2d Managing student behavior

  2e Organizing physical space

Domain 3: Instruction

  3a Communicating with students

  3b Using questioning and discussion techniques

  3c Engaging students in learning

  3d Providing feedback to students

  3e Demonstrating flexibility and responsiveness

Domain 4: Professional responsibilities

  4a Reflecting on teaching

  4b Maintaining accurate records

  4c Communicating with families

  4d Participating in the professional community

  4e Growing and developing professionally

  4f Showing professionalism

Source: Danielson 1996.

Table A.2 Summary Statistics

	Obs.	Mean	Standard deviation	Min	Max
Principal monitoring index	297	7.236	1.602	2	11
Creating an environment of respect and rapport	311	1.171	0.413	0	2
Providing feedback to students	291	1.830	0.699	0	3
Designing student assessment	305	2.243	1.421	0	6
Designing coherent instruction	305	0.243	0.429	0	1
Teacher level of education	305	2.089	0.665	1	5
Reading preservice training	305	0.377	0.485	0	1
Math preservice training	305	0.384	0.487	0	1
Receipt of external funding	311	0.174	0.379	0	1
Households with computer	311	0.644	0.223	0	1
School wealth index	311	−0.001	0.720	−5.161	0.582
Directorate school inspection	311	1.865	0.737	0	3
Directorate supervisor classroom visit	304	1.174	1.074	0	4
Parent–teacher association meeting frequency	309	2.058	0.740	0	4
rural	311	0.399	0.490	0	1
Log (teacher–student ratio)	304	3.175	0.469	1.099	3.892
School gender	311	0.900	0.647	0	2

Table A.3 Principal Monitoring and Teacher Effort in Jordan

	Providing feedback to students			Creating a climate of respect			Designing student assessments			Designing coherent instruction		
	Model 1	Model 2	Model 3	Model 4	Model 5	Model 6	Model 7	Model 8	Model 9	Model 10	Model 11	Model 12
Principal monitoring index	0.058**	0.062**	0.064**	0.024*	0.025*	0.023*	0.043	0.040	0.043	0.017	0.016	0.022*
	(0.025)	(0.025)	(0.026)	(0.014)	(0.014)	(0.014)	(0.027)	(0.027)	(0.027)	(0.012)	(0.012)	(0.12)
School gender	−0.054	−0.064	−0.021	0.090***	0.087***	0.114***	0.084	0.082	0.092	0.012	0.010	0.014
	(0.057)	(0.057)	(0.059)	(0.032)	(0.032)	(0.033)	(0.061)	(0.069)	(0.061)	(0.027)	(0.027)	(0.028)
Rural	−0.052	−0.032	−0.059	0.105***	0.105***	0.077	0.101	0.097	0.102	0.087*	0.084*	0.094**
	(0.092)	(0.092)	(0.096)	(0.050)	(0.051)	(0.051)	(0.103)	(0.101)	(0.105)	(0.045)	(0.046)	(0.047)
Computer in household	0.353*	0.319	0.369*	−0.035	−0.041	−0.280	−0.077	−0.065	−0.155	0.074	0.072	0.075
	(0.209)	(0.207)	(0.206)	(0.115)	(0.115)	(0.112)	(0.222)	(0.219)	(0.219)	(0.100)	(0.100)	(0.101)
School wealth index	−0.126*	−0.118*	−0.129*	0.016	0.019	0.003	0.091	0.068	0.048	−0.030	−0.035	−0.032
	(0.066)	(0.065)	(0.066)	(0.034)	(0.034)	(0.034)	(0.065)	(0.065)	(0.066)	(0.029)	(0.030)	(0.030)
Receipt of external funding		0.127	0.141		0.038	0.031		0.140	0.133		0.047	0.048
		(0.111)	(0.111)		(0.063)	(0.061)		(0.121)	(0.120)		(0.055)	(0.55)
Reading preservice training		−0.211**	−0.228**		−0.017	−0.001		0.195*	0.182		0.047	0.047
		(0.105)	(0.105)		(0.060)	(0.059)		(0.113)	(0.113)		(0.052)	(0.052)
Math preservice Training		0.196*	0.197*		−0.017	−0.024		0.094	0.089		−0.009	−0.024
		(0.105)	(0.105)		(0.060)	(0.059)		(0.112)	(0.111)		(0.052)	(0.052)
Directorate supervisor classroom visit			0.070			0.076***			0.046			−0.026
			(0.043)			(0.023)			(0.046)			(0.021)
Log (teacher–student ratio)			−0.100			−0.012			0.047			0.078
			(0.099)			(0.059)			(0.107)			(0.049)
Teacher education			0.094			0.050			0.066			0.028
			(0.059)			(0.032)			(0.059)			(0.028)
Directorate school inspection			−0.020			−0.099***			−0.032			−0.035
			(0.064)			(0.035)			(0.074)			(0.033)

table continues next page

101

Table A.3 Principal Monitoring and Teacher Effort in Jordan (continued)

	Providing feedback to students			Creating a climate of respect			Designing student assessments			Designing coherent instruction		
	Model 1	Model 2	Model 3	Model 4	Model 5	Model 6	Model 7	Model 8	Model 9	Model 10	Model 11	Model 12
Parent–teacher association meeting frequency			−0.054			0.001			0.061			−0.025
			(0.056)			(0.031)			(0.060)			(0.028)
Constant	1.234***	1.210***	1.346***	0.891***	0.902***	0.923***	1.716***	1.592***	1.234**	0.062	0.047	−0.158
	(0.259)	(0.258)	(0.421)	(0.143)	(0.144)	(0.232)	(0.329)	(0.331)	(0.480)	(0.131)	(0.132)	(0.209)
Directorates	39	39	39	39	39	38	39	39	38	39	39	38
Schools	149	149	147	152	152	150	152	152	150	152	152	150
N	276	276	273	293	293	289	293	293	289	293	293	289

Note: Standard errors appear in parentheses.

*p < .10; **p < .05; ***p < .01.

Table A.4 Summary Statistics of Variables Included in the Mediation Analysis

Variable	Obs.	Mean	Standard deviation	Min	Max
Letter sound knowledge	3,063	26.167	21.344	0	100
Reading comprehension	2,832	33.439	31.513	0	100
Number identification	2,987	77.349	24.829	0	100
Word problems	3,063	1.224	1.039	0	3
Creating a climate of respect and rapport	2,882	1.171	0.563	0	2
Providing feedback to students	2,582	1.871	0.838	0	3
Designing student assessments	3,003	2.241	1.426	0	6
Designing coherent instruction	3,003	0.246	0.431	0	1
Monitoring index	2,923	7.229	1.602	2	11
Help with homework	3,063	0.872	0.334	0	1
Private tutoring sessions	3,052	0.336	0.916	0	3
Radio in household	3,063	0.473	0.499	0	1
Vehicle in household	3,063	0.708	0.455	0	1
Computer in household	3,043	1.584	2.072	0	5
Receive free meals	3,063	0.645	0.479	0	1

Table A.5 The Indirect Effect of Principal Monitoring on Student Outcomes

	Dependent variable			
Mediating variable	Letter sound knowledge	Reading comprehension	Number identification	Word problems
Providing feedback to students	0.009** (0.04)	0.007*** (0.01)	0.005* (0.08)	0.003* (0.09)
Creating an environment of respect and rapport	0.003** (0.04)	0.012*** (0.01)	0.009*** (0.00)	0.008*** (0.01)
Designing student assessments	0.002 (0.16)	0.003 (0.15)	0.004** (0.03)	0.003** (0.03)
Designing coherent instruction	−0.001 (0.74)	0.001 (0.69)	0.001 (0.36)	−0.002 (0.62)

Note: The p values appear in parentheses.
*p = .9; **p = .95; ***p = .99.

Table A.6 Robustness Checks on the Indirect Effect of Principal Monitoring on Student Outcomes

	Dependent variable			
Mediating variable	Letter sound knowledge	Reading comprehension	Number identification	Word problems
Providing feedback to students	0.026*** (0.00)	0.028*** (0.00)	0.023*** (0.00)	0.018*** (0.00)
Creating an environment of respect and rapport	0.004* (0.08)	0.007* (0.09)	0.007** (0.03)	0.005** (0.05)
Designing student assessments	0.003 (0.17)	0.004 (0.16)	0.005*** (0.01)	0.005* (0.07)
Designing coherent instruction	−0.013 (0.33)	−0.014 (0.38)	−0.017 (0.14)	−0.025* (0.09)

Note: The p values appear in parentheses.
*p = .9; **p = .95; ***p = .99.

Sensitivity Analysis.

The sequential ignorability (SI) assumption is necessary to achieve identification in mediation analysis. The SI assumption comprises two assumptions: first, the independent variable is assumed to be statistically independent of potential outcomes and potential mediating variables; and second, the mediating variable is assumed to be exogenous conditional on pretreatment confounders and the independent variable of interest (Hicks and Tingley 2011; see chapter 2 references). Since SI is likely to be violated in the data, a sensitivity analysis is presented in this appendix to determine the extent to which the estimates are robust to violations of SI.

The sensitivity parameter produced by sensitivity analysis—denoted by $\rho \in [-1, 1]$—represents the correlation between the error terms in the mediation and outcome models. A nonzero correlation between the error terms denotes a violation of the SI assumption. By conducting sensitivity analysis, the point for ρ where the indirect effect is estimated to be zero is calculated to determine how robust the estimates are to violations of SI.

For example, figure B.1 presents results from a sensitivity analysis that uses the letter sound knowledge variable to measure student outcomes and the providing feedback to students variable to proxy for teacher effort. The black line in the plot represents the estimated indirect effect (denoted by ACME) for different values of ρ. The sensitivity analysis estimates that the indirect effect is equal to 0 when ρ equals 0.1577; hence, the plot in the figure crosses 0 when ρ equals 0.1577. The 95 percent confidence interval around the estimated indirect effect at different values of ρ is denoted in gray. This suggests that the estimate of the indirect effect of principal monitoring is somewhat sensitive to violations of SI. Only when $\rho < 0.1$ is the indirect effect estimated to be positive and statistically significant. The results in the figure are highly representative of the results produced by sensitivity analyses for each of the 16 estimates presented in table A.5, suggesting that all of the results presented in this section are somewhat sensitive to SI violations.

Figure B.1 Sensitivity Analysis Results

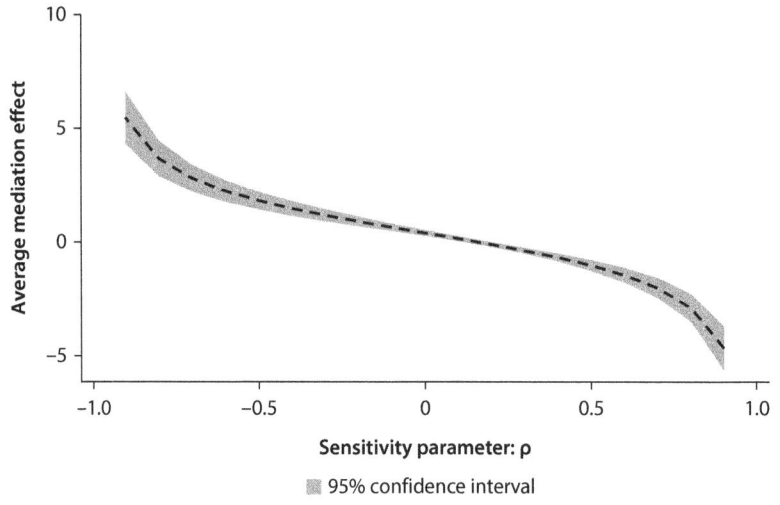

Health Sector

Sample Size Calculations

Because of a lack of preliminary data, sample size calculations relied on prior research examining the linkage between accountability and absenteeism (Banerjee, Duflo, and Glennerster 2008; D'Amuri 2011; Dhaliwal and Hanna 2014). Sample size calculation parameters include an alpha of 0.05, a power of 0.80, and the use of a linear regression model to test the primary relationship of interest in which provider effort, y, is regressed on approximately 15 independent variables $(x_1 - x_{15})$. The independent variable of interest x_i is assumed to increase the model's R^2 by 0.15 when it is included in the model and the restricted model's R^2 is assumed to be 0.1. The assumed intraclass correlation is 0.2, and the sample averages 10 primary health care centers per Directorate of Health in Jordan. On the basis of these assumptions, the study requires a sample size of approximately 120 primary health care centers across all 13 directorates of health. Assuming a continuous measure of provider effort based upon dichotomous ratings of provider effort at the patient level, a 90 percent confidence level, a margin of error no larger than 0.15, and that approximately 70 percent of patients will report that their physician provided high effort, then 25 patients should be surveyed at each facility. Budgetary constraints precluded a larger sample size, which would have reduced the margin of error.

Statistical Analyses

Descriptive statistics were generated to examine the distribution of the various measures of provider effort and the use of sanctions. In addition, the relationship among the provider effort variables was examined with a correlation matrix to understand how strongly the variables relate to one another and to ensure that they are not so highly correlated as to be substitutes for one another. To examine the relationship between accountability and provider effort, multilevel linear regression models allowed the intercept in the regression equation to vary randomly by Directorate of Health, as the clinics are nested within each directorate. Two models were constructed for each of the four measures of provider effort (absenteeism, compliance with CPGs, provision of rights-based care, and time with provider). In the first model for each of these outcomes (a), within-facility monitoring, sanctions, and rewards were modeled along with potential confounders. In the second model (b) for each outcome, an interaction between within-facility monitoring and sanctions was tested. Tests for an interaction between monitoring and incentives were originally intended, but the extremely skewed distribution of the nonfinancial incentives (that is, the vast majority of clinics did not have a positive incentive environment) precluded such a test. Estimated margins were calculated and graphed for the 25th, 50th, and 75th percentiles of the monitoring variable to display significant interactions. To examine whether the relationship between each outcome variable and the continuous exposure and confounder variables was linear, restricted cubic spline functions (Desquilbet and Mariotti 2010) were used and quadratic terms were introduced where indicated.

Regression Results

Table C.1 presents the results of the multilevel regression analysis where each within-facility accountability mechanism (monitoring, sanctions, and rewards) was examined for its independent relationship to provider effort. Statistical significance is indicated by (*), where (***) indicates a p value less than 0.01, (**) indicates a p value less than 0.05, and (*) indicates a p value less than 0.10. Standard errors for the estimated coefficients are in parentheses under each estimate. For a verbal description of the results see chapter 3.

Table C.1 Relationship between Accountability Practices and Provider Effort (N = 122)
b/se

Accountability practices	Absenteeism	Clinical effort	Rights-based practice	Time with a provider
CMO monitoring	−0.008	0.510***	0.278**	1.314**
	(0.029)	(0.163)	(0.122)	(0.572)
CMO sanctions	0.013	−0.546**	−0.500***	−0.120
	(0.039)	(0.224)	(0.167)	(0.787)
CMO rewards	−0.014	−0.228	−0.131	−1.163
	(0.035)	(0.206)	(0.153)	(0.732)
Top-down monitoring	0.017	−0.075	−0.095*	−0.619**
	(0.013)	(0.073)	(0.054)	(0.259)
Top-down sanctions	−0.027**	−0.080	−0.054	1.891**
	(0.013)	(0.078)	(0.058)	(0.865)
Top-down sanctions[a]				−0.570***
				(0.204)
Community health committee	−0.016	0.015	0.239*	0.773
	(0.030)	(0.173)	(0.129)	(0.600)
Socioeconomic status	0.005	2.753**	1.415	0.592
	(0.020)	(1.253)	(0.934)	(0.421)

table continues next page

Table C.1 Relationship between Accountability Practices and Provider Effort (N = 122) *(continued)*

	Absenteeism	Clinical effort	Rights-based practice	Time with a provider
Socioeconomic status		−0.236**	−0.113	
		(0.115)	(0.086)	
Preventive care	−0.211**	−0.192	0.388	2.653
	(0.102)	(0.570)	(0.425)	(2.035)
Patient health	−0.028	0.856***	0.386**	1.292*
	(0.034)	(0.203)	(0.153)	(0.719)
Provider continuing education	0.016	0.300	0.230	1.418
	(0.046)	(0.279)	(0.209)	(0.987)
CMO postgraduate training	0.015	0.109	−0.011	−1.211*
	(0.032)	(0.184)	(0.138)	(0.644)
Accreditation	−0.004	0.221	0.093	1.255**
	(0.031)	(0.174)	(0.130)	(0.611)
_cons	0.270	−6.491*	0.887	4.721
	(0.174)	(3.538)	(2.633)	(3.625)
Number of directorates	13	13	13	13
Number of primary health care centers	122	122	121	122

Note: Standard errors are shown in parentheses, and those that are statistically significant are marked with asterisks.
CMO = chief medical officer.

References

Banerjee, Abhijit V., Esther Duflo, and Rachel Glennerster. 2008. "Putting a Band-Aid on a Corpse: Incentives for Nurses in the Indian Public Health Care System." *Journal of the European Economic Association* 6: 487–500.

Danielson, Charlotte. 2011. *Enhancing Professional Practice: A Framework for Teaching.* Alexandria, VA: Association for Supervision and Curriculum Development.

D'Amuri, Francesco. 2011. "Monetary Incentives vs. Monitoring in Addressing Absenteeism: Experimental Evidence." Bank of Italy, Economic Research and International Relations Area, Rome.

Desquilbet, Loic, and François Mariotti. 2010. "Dose Response Analyses using Restricted Cubic Spline Functions in Public Health Research." *Statistics in Medicine* 29 (9): 1037–57.

Dhaliwal, Iqbal, and Rema Hanna. 2014. "Deal with the Devil: The Successes and Limitations of Bureaucratic Reform in India." National Bureau of Economic Research, Cambridge, MA.

Environmental Benefits Statement

The World Bank Group is committed to reducing its environmental footprint. In support of this commitment, we leverage electronic publishing options and print-on-demand technology, which is located in regional hubs worldwide. Together, these initiatives enable print runs to be lowered and shipping distances decreased, resulting in reduced paper consumption, chemical use, greenhouse gas emissions, and waste.

We follow the recommended standards for paper use set by the Green Press Initiative. The majority of our books are printed on Forest Stewardship Council (FSC)–certified paper, with nearly all containing 50–100 percent recycled content. The recycled fiber in our book paper is either unbleached or bleached using totally chlorine-free (TCF), processed chlorine–free (PCF), or enhanced elemental chlorine–free (EECF) processes.

More information about the Bank's environmental philosophy can be found at http://www.worldbank.org/corporateresponsibility.

green press INITIATIVE

www.ingramcontent.com/pod-product-compliance
Lightning Source LLC
Chambersburg PA
CBHW082104210326
41599CB00033B/6580